# Caddell Dry Dock:
// 100 Years Harborside

Caddell Dry Dock:
100 Years Harborside

by Erin Urban

with contemporary photographs by Michael Falco

The Noble Maritime Collection
Staten Island, New York, *Publisher*

Front cover: A shipyard worker descending from a tug in dry dock.

Back cover: The tug *Mister T* in dry dock #3 with the tug *Barbara E. Bouchard* behind her in dry dock #7.

Frontispiece: Working through the night, a yard welder is fabricating new steel shelves for the bow fenders of the tug *Barbara E. Bouchard*, in dry dock #7 behind him.

PHOTOS: Michael Falco

FIRST EDITION
Copyright 2009, The Noble Maritime Collection
All rights reserved including the right of reproduction in whole or in part in any form

Published by the Noble Maritime Collection, Staten Island, New York

Edited by Jill Cutler and Kris Fresonke

Designed by Ciro Galeno, Jr.

Printed by Permanent Printing, Ltd., China

Library of Congress Cataloguing-in-Publication Data

Urban, Erin, 1948-
      Caddell Dry Dock: 100 Years Harborside
Caddell Dry Dock and Repair Company / Erin Urban
      P. cm.
      Includes index
      ISBN 978-0-9623017-3-5
       1. Caddell Dry Dock and Repair Company 2. Maritime businesses— United States 3. Dry docking

*Dedicated to the men and women of
Caddell Dry Dock and Repair Company*

Contents

Introduction ix
by John B. Caddell II, *Chairman and CEO, Caddell Dry Dock and Repair Company*

Foreword xi
by Peter Stanford, *President* emeritus, *National Maritime Historical Society*

The Company & Its History 1

Dry Docking 49

Portrait of a Dry Dock 61
An essay in photographs by Michael Falco

Bibliography and List of Sources 105

Acknowledgements 107

Index 109

About the Author 113

Introduction

A view of shipyard activities; *from the left*, a bit of dry dock #1, one of the last wood dry docks operating in the world; the tug *Craig Reinauer* on dry dock #8, Caddell's new dry dock; the yard tug, *LW Caddell*, towing a pontoon with a spudded barge in the foreground. *In the distance to the right*, the tug *Rhea I. Bouchard*, in front of her, the new tug *Morton S. Bouchard* and the supply boat *Evening Star*; on the pier, the crane *Claude Forbes*, a bit of dry dock #2, and the yard tug *Jay Bee V* being overhauled.
PHOTO: Michael Falco

Introduction
by John B. Caddell II *Chairman and CEO, Caddell Dry Dock and Repair Company*

A few years ago Erin Urban asked me if I wanted her to write a book about the history of the Caddell Dry Dock and Repair Co., Inc. My first response was a very respectable, "probably not." Then followed a few months of appeals, some from Erin, some from Peter Stanford, some from our President, Steve Kalil, and there were others. Erin assured me that if she wrote the book the process would be interesting, fun, and not obtrusive, and the rest argued, successfully, that any privately owned and operated business that made it past the 100 year mark should be commemorated.

So here we have it: *Caddell Dry Dock: 100 years Harborside*! With a lot of help we collected old historical notes, papers, pictures, and, along with some very old memories, Erin very carefully and artfully weaved them together in writing this book. I can only be saddened, however, that because of fires at the shipyard many wonderful artifacts were lost over the years that would have been useful to her work and undoubtedly would have enhanced the book.

My gratitude is abundant to all the people that worked hard to bring this book to life. I am also very grateful to have worked with, and still have, a loyal and hard-working core of employees, without which, we certainly would never have made it this far. All our customers, most assuredly, have been our lifeblood, and all of us at Caddell's owe them our gratitude for their trust and support.

Since I became president in 1966 I have seen over twenty shipyards in New York Harbor close shop. Thankfully, with much support and probably a lot of luck, we are still standing, almost alone, in New York Harbor, ready to take on any new challenges in the business of dry docking and repairing our customer's vessels. It has and always will be an honor to do so. Thank you all.

Shackles and chain falls, age-old tools in a shipyard.
PHOTO: Michael Falco

Foreword

by Peter Stanford *President emeritus, National Maritime Historical Society*

In 2003 Caddell Dry Dock & Repair celebrated its 100th anniversary as the oldest, largest, and most technologically advanced shipyard in New York. In a city perhaps not aware of the armadas of coastal and international trade that stream through its harbor—which carries nine-tenths of the foreign traffic—the Noble Maritime Collection decided on a close-up look at how this big and progressive shipyard functions. In their usual style, Noble Maritime took it on themselves to tell this story through direct, personal accounts of the people who made Caddell's the leading ship repair facility in New York.

The Noble Maritime Collection, set up in the classic old sailors' home called Sailors' Snug Harbor in Staten Island, was founded in 1987 to celebrate the work of the great harbor artist John A. Noble (1913-83), and to educate New Yorkers and all comers in the hardworking world of harbor people, whose lives he shared and expressed in memorable paintings and lithographs.

Some people thought the Noble Maritime effort to celebrate Caddell's was not going to cause much of a stir among "seen-it-all" New Yorkers—but they couldn't have been more wrong. The exhibition presented the bare bottoms of huge vessels out of water during repairs needed for their next voyage, powerful tugs getting new shafts to deliver the pull that hauls barges carrying much more than a hundred highway-clogging, sky-polluting trucks, and intimate pictorial accounts of how the ailing innards and sometimes the ruptured outer skins of these vessels are quickly and accurately repaired—so that any ship putting into Caddell's leaves in sound, reliable condition.

But that is only the flowering of the story, fascinating as it was to young and old, who came in droves to point out items to each other which had been carefully selected and honed to cut to the heart of the action, a show only a team deeply versed in the subject could have put on. Ah, but the roots—perhaps I shall be forgiven for saying the grassroots—of this story were a step beyond anything made of wood or metal.

These were the people of Caddell's, in all their rich variety, bringing a wide-ranging array of skills to bear on the highly individual problems of the ships that come in for repair. And they bring more than that, a united spirit and a way of going at things that extends from top to bottom of the company roster, currently some 200 souls. They are the reason that Caddell's has forged ahead while over the past half-century, over 30 working shipyards in the harbor have gone out of business. More to the point, they are the reason that Caddell's

Foreword

Foreword

Aerial view of Caddell Dry Dock and Repair Company, 1987; *from the lower left*, the Marine Power and Light Boat Yard, H & R Dry Dock Company, Caddell's Main Yard, Penn Maritime Transportation Company, and Caddell's East Yard

PHOTO: Bill Higgins, Collection of Caddell Dry Dock and Repair Company

future looks so bright, a future which will hold challenges demanding innovative responses.

In this exhibition one got this message, so by the time you came to the great floor-to-ceiling photos of the employees, you were interested enough to stop and see which faces you could recognize. Kent Barwick, president of the Municipal Art Society, got word of these portraits of Caddell's workers and the gigantic group portrait on the back of a tugboat, and from his midtown office aerie in Manhattan he reached out to bring the whole exhibition to the center of New York City. This was the first time the venerable society, founded in 1892, had featured such a gritty industrial subject—and Kent reports it was an immediate attraction for people who did not know the hidden life that keeps New York viable as a center of trade.

How this happened is a story in itself, a story that begins with John B. Caddell leaving his Canadian home at the head of the Gulf of Maine, where wooden schooners came in at high tide to run aground, and workers came out at low tide to cure the aging ships of whatever ailed them. You don't go into business in the well-traveled schooner community without getting to know about the world around you, even many miles away, and John Bartlett Caddell learned early that whereas the old schooner trades were dying out in rockbound harbors of New England and Canada's Maritime Provinces, the action was lively and growing in the great American harbors to the south, notably in New York Harbor.

As the 1800s ended, the maritime world was going through epochal change. For five thousand years mankind had made long passages under sail, and now this was coming to an end, as more and more steamers took over. In the British merchant marine, at that time the world's greatest, steamers puffing away in their iron hulls had begun to outweigh the tonnage of merchant commerce still under sail as early as 1885. In the United States, in the State of Maine particularly, rugged Yankee captains, shipbuilders and traders went on building great wooden schooners, some of over 5,000 tons, or bigger than the average steamer, and young men joined their forebears to sail them. But the handwriting was on the wall, and by 1905, there was a greater tonnage of steamers than sailing ships under the American flag.

By that time, John Caddell had gotten his footing in New York, and with the support of ship-owners who liked his work, had opened his own yard in Brooklyn. During the rush of shipping business in the buildup to World War I, he found himself crowded out of the busy Erie Basin, where bigger companies were expanding. In 1916, with the support of Berwind White Coal Company, whose owners wanted to see this able and conscientious shipwright continue in business, he moved his yard to the north shore of Staten Island, on the busy Kill van Kull, the waterway which separates Staten Island from New Jersey. He established his company on land which a vastly expanded enterprise still occupies today.

Staten Island's shores were alive with shipyards, and had been so almost from the beginning of their settlement. When JB, as Caddell was called, first came down from Canada, he worked as dockmaster at Burlee Shipyard in Port Richmond; Burlee's was a shipbuilding yard with one railway that built tugboats. The last tug constructed there was the *EJ Berwind*, launched in 1902. JB met John Van Wee at Burlee's; he was the manager of Berwind's marine operations in New York, which included over 300 coal barges and two tugboats, the *EJ Berwind* and *Admiral Dewey*. Van Wee took a liking to the young Canadian and encouraged him to go into business for himself—so he could take care of the Berwind account.

When Van Wee died, Charles E. Dunlap, president of Berwind's, asked JB to find a replacement, and JB did—Captain William French, a master aboard a large steam yacht, became the manager of the firm's New York operations. Their friendship cemented a long association between Caddell and Berwind White—not only had the company loaned him the money to buy his Staten Island yard, they were its main customer.

Foreword

America was going through a monumental change in this era, in the shift from an economy and society dominated by farming, to the industrial and commercial behemoth which the world recognizes, friend and foe alike, as one of the wonders of the modern world. By 1917, as John Caddell was making his way in his new Staten Island yard, American steel production—a key indicator of national wealth and power in those days—had risen to 25.8 million tons, more than the combined production of Britain, long the leading industrial power, which produced 9.9 million tons and the rising power of Germany, at 12.7 million tons.

From the start, Caddell's did much more than dry docking. JB built coal barges for Berwind and manufactured and repaired mechanical parts and equipment, from steel pistons to connecting rods, using wooden patterns from which the parts were cast at the shipyard. His metal working facilities made replacement fittings of all sorts, first for the lofty rigs of the great coastal schooners, and later for the boilers and engines of steam-powered vessels. The centuries-old prevalence of sail on the world's oceans and waterways was coming to an end. At Caddell's, the transition was seamless. The company adapted to its new materials and methods, and advanced the craft of building ships and manufacturing parts.

But JB's grandson, John Bartlett Caddell II, still fondly remembers the Age of Steam—"the quiet swish of steam as vessels slipped into the shipyard, the meticulous crews of those immaculate boats, and the lingering aroma of moist steam." Caddell's worked on steam engines until the mid 1960s. The *Esso #7* and *#8* were the last steam tugs they repaired, and the *Hightstown* and *Blairstown* were the last stick lighters to come into the yard. By the end of the decade, the diesel engine had supplanted steam once and for all.

The story, as you can follow it in this lively and authentic account of the Caddell yard, is one of steady organic growth through rapidly changing times and work practices. There have been no takeovers of the firm, no gigantic infusions of cash—capital has grown through steadily accumulating profits and practical business sense. To the west of Caddell's was Larsen's Shipyard and to the east was Brighton Marine Shipyard. Over the years Caddell's has incorporated both and integrated the company ethos of individual initiative, responsibility, and cooperation.

John B. Caddell II, president from 1966 until 1988 when he became chairman, is conscious of his grandfather's principles, based on respect for the individual and on the development of a work force made up of people able to perform a variety of different jobs and trained to achieve consistently high standards in each. This approach to work force development has been hailed as a management revolution in recent years. But the approach was not new at Caddell's, and moguls of industry could well have learned it much earlier at the shipyard. If they could have made their way down to the Caddell yard on the

Kill van Kull and put themselves through the apprenticeship that the company's president, Steve Kalil, was put through when he joined the yard as a carpenter in 1975, they may have adapted the approach sooner. Kalil's first job at the yard was to make his own wooden toolbox. It had to have mortises and tenons and all its seams so tight—without caulking—that it could have sailed across the Kill without leaking a drop of water. As president Kalil has come to understand every aspect of the shipyard, down to the smallest detail.

The yard, as you will read, is ahead of the game in automated welding and steel shaping and the use of new materials—but there is nothing automated about the individual approach given to each ship that enters the yard. The sea is unforgiving to those who think foolproof systems solve all problems. There have to be people deeply invested in those systems to make them workable in traversing an element that will ruthlessly seek out every ill-conceived shortcut or "good enough" solution to the individual problems that every ship repair presents.

I have some personal knowledge of this, for the 2,200-ton iron square-rigger *Wavertree* of 1885, on whose restoration I had worked many weekends as a volunteer, went to Caddell's to get her new rig—executed to half-forgotten designs, in outmoded shapes. Caddell's brought a 69-year old ironworker out of retirement to make her 80 and 90 foot yard arms. She came home ready to meet the unchanging sea as she entered the new millennium, in a world incredibly changed from the one in which she was launched. Other historic ships you'll find in these pages have been similarly well treated, matching old designs generated in distant places with no surviving witnesses to explain how it was all done.

It seemed to me and others that the story needed telling in book form, so I was especially pleased when John Caddell agreed to the publication of the story, with which he cooperated in every way. And Erin Urban at the Noble Maritime Collection went to work with the staff and devoted volunteers to produce the volume you have before you.

A special touch was brought to the story by the sensitive and gifted photographer Michael Falco, whose account of his own experience getting to know the people in the Caddell yard adds the excitement of an artistic vision taking shape in the milieu of plain-spoken people expressing in words and action what their complex and difficult work is about.

In a time of changing and sometimes confused values, it is reassuring to encounter a company like Caddell's, whose word has ever been its bond and which is in business for the long haul. In Erin's book about a business whose people and principles she knows and so clearly admires, I believe you'll find your exploration of a modern shipyard a rewarding experience.

Foreword

The tug *Mister T* in dry dock #3 with the *Barbara E. Bouchard* behind her in dry dock #7.
PHOTO: Michael Falco

The Company & Its History

Caddell Dry Dock: 100 Years Harborside

Previous page: A worker on dry dock #7.
PHOTO: Michael Falco

The Company & Its History

Aerial view of Caddell Dry Dock and Repair Company; 2005; *from lower left*, a Bouchard tank barge, tied up; a Bouchard tank barge and tug; the Staten Island ferry *Andrew J. Barberi* in dry dock #6 in Caddell's East Yard; Caddell's main yard; Marine Power and Light Company; the NYC Department of Environmental Protection Sewage Treatment Plant

PHOTO: Michael Falco

The 100-year history of Caddell Dry Dock and Repair Company spans the last century, a period which saw the great transition from sail to steam in the maritime industry. Yet the world of Caddell Dry Dock in 1903 was in many ways no different from its world today. The way the yard hums, the way it works, the way it has to work—that harmony of labor and rhythm—has not changed. The basic elements of shipbuilding and repair, namely fire, water, wood, and metal, and the craftsmanship inherent in mastering and fashioning those elements, have not changed. The yard's values—impeccable standards, graciousness to customers, support of employees—are as strong as they were in 1888, when John Bartlett Caddell put his tool chest on his back and left Maple Grove, Nova Scotia, to seek a way to capitalize on his knowledge of shipbuilding.

Caddell Dry Dock and Repair Company is not only the oldest shipyard in New York Harbor, it is also one of the last. It has survived wars, terrorism, competition, strikes, fires, and a more recent affliction—government regulation. Father has passed it on to son for three generations. Its operation a century later boasts six dry docks, which annually refurbish over 300 ships. It is one of New York's most venerable family firms. And that is the way its founder, John B. Caddell, wanted it. Not only did he understand shipbuilding, he knew that water and weather take their toll on a vessel, and it is easier and faster to maintain existing ships than to build new ones.

Sailing vessels at low tide in the Bay of Fundy, a natural dry dock.
PHOTO: E. Graham, Collection of Conger Reynolds, Courtesy of Nova Scotia Archives and Records Management

Born on the family farm in Maple Grove, Nova Scotia in 1866, John B. Caddell, known throughout his life as JB, was the youngest of five sons. While his brothers went to sea and became ship captains, he worked the family farm and apprenticed at the Lawrence Shipyard in Maitland, on the Bay of Fundy. Perhaps it was the way that vast bay empties at low tide—setting schooners in the mud in a natural dry dock, until the great bore comes rushing in and sets them afloat again—that led him to become a shipbuilder.

JB's oldest brother, William, died young, and the four remaining Caddell brothers married the four Forbes daughters, who lived across the road from their farm. The Caddell farm provided vegetables and meat for the family and villagers, and included an apple orchard. From his neighbor's five daughters, JB chose Annie Forbes as his bride.

As he matured, he watched the wooden ship industry in Maitland decline, when the advent of trucks, trains, and steam and diesel-powered vessels drew the industry away from the swifter, more economical wooden ship. He realized he had to seek work in Boston or New York but first tried his luck in Salem, Massachusetts. He quickly moved on to the busy port of New York, where he

The Windsor Plaster Mill, 1891, with one of the Gypsum Fleet schooners, most likely the *Gypsum Queen*, tied up at the wharf. Many Nova Scotians traveled aboard the *Queen* to New York in the winter to work in shipyards and returned home on her in the spring to work their farms. US Gypsum bought the Windsor site in 1924, and in 1976 sold it to the Atlantic Salt Company, which today uses it for salt storage and distribution. PHOTO: USG

worked at Tiejan & Lang Shipyard, the forerunner of Todd Shipyard. Later he worked as a ship's carpenter and dry dock master at the Burlee Dry Dock Company in Port Richmond and at Staten Island Shipbuilding, the predecessor of the Bethlehem Steel Shipbuilding Division.

JB's brother-in-law, Wentworth Forbes, a carriage maker, followed him south. Each year for the next twelve years, the two men journeyed by steamboat in the fall to work in shipyards, and returned home to Nova Scotia to their farms and families in the spring. They often sailed on the *Gypsum Queen*. She transported gypsum, a mineral used to make plaster, from Halifax, Nova Scotia to the Windsor Plaster Mill on Staten Island, on Richmond Terrace. The site of the original gypsum plant is on the north shore of Staten Island, at the mouth of the Kill van Kull, the waterway that separates Staten Island from New Jersey.

In 1903 JB met his future partners— Eugene Schuyler, a salesman, and John Payne, an accountant—and went into partnership to form Schuyler, Payne & Caddell, a ship repair company. They rented a shipyard with two large railways, one 150 feet and the other 250 feet long, and a 130-foot long dry dock, at Van Dyke Street in the Red Hook section of Brooklyn.

The yard prospered. Payne in due course left the firm, and in 1912, JB and Schuyler moved their operation to the Erie Basin in Brooklyn. They doubled their size when

The family of John Bartlett Caddell c. 1900
From top left, his wife, the former Annie Forbes; their daughter Lillian; and JB himself; and their children, *from the bottom left*, Beatrice, Leroy, and Laura
PHOTO: Collection of John B. Caddell II

Four views of the Schulyer, Payne & Caddell yard at Erie Basin, Brooklyn, c. 1910

Top left: Typical bulwark damage on a wooden tug, c. 1930

Bottom left: The Ward Line stick lighter *Eastport of New York*, left, at the Erie Basin yard, c. 1910. The covered barge *Export of New York* is beside her. The freighter *Saluda* and a steamship are in the background at right. A three-masted schooner is behind the stick lighter at left.

Top right: The New York & Cuba Mail Steamship Company covered barge *Export of New York* tied up at the Erie Basin Yard, c. 1910. She carried cargo from Cuba that was unloaded in New York Harbor. Beside her are two tugs, and behind them, to the right, are the freighters *Saluda* and *Lake Elsinore*.

Bottom right: Side view of the *Eastport of New York* with the freighter *Saluda* and a four-masted schooner behind her.

PHOTOS: Collection of Caddell Dry Dock and Repair Company

they purchased a second dry dock from the Hildebrant Dry Dock Company in South Rondout, New York, and opened as Schuyler and Caddell. Eugene Schuyler had no experience in the operation of a shipyard, and spent his days in Manhattan drumming up business for the yard. In 1914, JB bought out his share of the partnership, took over all aspects of its operations, and formed John B. Caddell Dry Dock Company. His family had grown, and with Annie and their five children—Lillian, Leroy, Laura, Beatrice, and Marjean—he settled on Shore Road and 85th Street in Bay Ridge, Brooklyn.

City plans in 1915 to rebuild the Erie Basin, a defunct ferry depot, and put in piers for larger ships forced JB to seek a new location. Fearing for the shipyard's livelihood, its prime customer, the Berwind White Coal Company, lent him the tugboat *Admiral Dewey*, and he steamed around New York Harbor looking for a place to set up a new yard.

On the Staten Island side of the Kill van Kull, he came upon the remains of John Starin's old side-wheel steamer and excursion boat shipyard off Broadway, in an area of graceful, tree-lined streets and grand Victorian homes. The terminal was defunct, and the property cluttered with the sunken hulls of old wooden steamers and excursion boats. He decided it would suit his needs and took a 5-year, interest-free loan of $300,000 from Berwind's to buy it. Late in 1916 he set up the new headquarters of the John B. Caddell Dry Dock Company at the foot of Broadway, Staten Island, where it still is today.

The Caddell Family home at 147 85th Street in the Bay Ridge section of Brooklyn had ten rooms, three baths, and a two-car garage. JB and Annie raised their burgeoning family of five in the spacious house overlooking New York Bay.
PHOTO: Courtesy Brian Merlis and Lee A. Rosenzweig

First JB built pier #1. Then he towed dry docks #1 and #2 from Brooklyn and installed them on either side of it. He built a machine shop, a carpenter's shop, a storeroom, and a building that housed a large coal-fired, water tube boiler and a steam air compressor that he used to power machinery and dry dock pumps throughout the shipyard. He installed heavy equipment and floating cranes, and he built a third dry dock.

The firm's largest client was still Berwind's, for whom Caddell's built and repaired coal barges. They also repaired and re-rigged commercial coastal schooners. To get schooner work, it was common for the shipyard to invest in a small "share" of the vessel, and during these early years, the yard's main building had an enormous slot through it to accommodate the bowsprit of the many wooden sailing ships that came into the yard.

In 1915, when he was forced to leave his Erie Basin yard, JB steamed around the Harbor in the *Admiral Dewey*, a tug lent to him by the Berwind White Coal Company.

PHOTO: Collection of Caddell Dry Dock and Repair Company

A clannish group, many of the early employees were JB's fellow Nova Scotians, experts in carpentry and rigging. Brother-in-law Wentworth Forbes brought his carpentry skills as carriage maker to make wooden patterns for metal castings of mechanical parts for both ships and dry docks, things like impellors, propellers, pumps, and pulleys. The largest gang early on was the wood workers and caulkers. The caulkers were mostly Italian immigrants, and the ship's carpenters were a mix of Nova Scotians and Norwegians.

In 1931, Claude, Wentworth's eager sixteen-year old son, took his first job at the yard for a wage of $.37 per hour. He stayed with Caddell's for 72 years, retiring in 2003. He remembers "the old *Stacey*—she had big old bowsprits used to come through the buildings."

Berwind's regularly brought in coke and unloaded it with a steam crane, and Claude bagged it and delivered what was not used at the yard to private houses in the neighborhood in a 1928 International flatbed truck. Over the years he learned to run cranes, run boats, run the storeroom, and, perhaps most significantly, he shaped the adolescent character and interests of JB's grandson and successor, John B. Caddell II.

JB built a business renowned for its standards and integrity. "A handshake

John Starin's shipyard at the foot of Broadway in Staten Island. The paddle-wheel steam excursion boats tied up at his wharf took New Yorkers on summer trips around the Harbor. JB bought the yard in 1915.
PHOTO: *Staten Island Advance*

was a contract," his grandson recalled, "and common sense prevailed." Loyal customers included Standard Oil, originally a Rockefeller holding, which later split into Socony (Standard Oil of New York) and Esso (Standard Oil of New Jersey). Socony transformed into Mobil, and Esso into Exxon, then merged again as Exxon Mobil, and Caddell's yard continues to be its home. Tracy Towing, handling most of the coal for Con Edison, was loyal, as was, of course, Berwind White. The Coast Guard began to use the facility. Another family member, Raymond Caddell, joined the firm around this time. The son of JB's brother Archibald, he was a dedicated and loyal employee and served in management positions for over forty years.

An honorable man, JB helped a number of people, lent money on a handshake and an IOU, and helped his employees build their homes on Staten Island. His grandson recalls a typical gesture on the part of his grandfather. Chauffeured each morning by car to the 69th Street Ferry in Brooklyn, JB got to know the ticket agent at the pier. One morning as he arrived, JB noticed that the agent looked forlorn and asked what was wrong. Learning that the gentleman's wife needed an operation, JB immediately gave him the necessary $2,000. The agent repaid the loan—and thereafter made sure JB always got his car on the ferry.

"JB," John Bartlett Caddell, 1928
PHOTO: Collection of Caddell Dry Dock and Repair Company

On September 16, 1920, JB was almost killed. An unknown person—a suspected member of the Anarchist Society, which was active in New York City at the time—set off a homemade bomb. The radical sent a horse-drawn cart filled with dynamite and sash weights down Wall Street, where JB was walking. The cart exploded near the intersection of Wall and Broad Streets. It killed 30 people instantly and injured about 300 others, 40 of whom later died from their injuries. JB was thrown across the street by the blast.

One eyewitness recalled a 100-foot mushroom-shaped cloud of smoke, licked by tongues of flame, filling the street with acrid smoke, shards of glass, and fire. Even people inside their offices were killed, as hundreds of pounds of sash weights flew through the air like shrapnel.

JB was severely injured. He spent several weeks in the hospital, and after he was released, he went to Florida to recuperate further. From then on he adopted the practice of wintering in Miami Beach. The experience on Wall Street seemed to have changed his habits and priorities. He slowed down and relished life more. Although he spent the spring and summer in Brooklyn on Shore Drive, he gradually withdrew from the day-to-day operations of the yard.

JB had been coincidentally involved in the worst act of terrorism in United States history until the September 11, 2001 attacks on the World Trade Center. On September 17, 1920, the day after the

The aftermath of the Wall Street bombing of September 16, 1920. PHOTO: U.S. Library of Congress

Wall Street bombing, a crowd gathered there, around the statue of George Washington, which had emerged miraculously undamaged. They listened to speakers blaming and decrying nameless radicals for the bombing, and they sang the *Star-Spangled Banner*. Throngs of people filled the narrow street, which had never before seen such numbers. Although Americans of the 1920s waited months, and then years, for the case to break, no one was ever caught.

In 1925, JB, who was 59, passed the dry dock reins to his only son, Leroy. He continued to watch over the company as Chairman and CEO, and Leroy, who had served in the U.S. Navy in World War I and was working at the yard, took over as president.

Leroy was the obvious choice to succeed his father. He was the family's only son; he was born to the shipbuilder's life, and

Young Naval engineer Leroy Caddell aboard the motor yacht, *Tarantula*, c. 1917
PHOTO: Collection of John B. Caddell II

he spent his youth around a shipyard. Born in 1896 on the family farm in Maple Grove, he was four years-old in 1900 when he sailed for the first time with his mother and older sister Lillian from Halifax to a pier on the east side of Manhattan. Annie was seasick for the entire trip, and he always remembered that. His father met them at the boat and took them to a small house he had rented at 56 Cary Avenue on Staten Island. His Dad was working at the Burlee Shipyard in Port Richmond, and Leroy remembered his "going to the shipyard and home by bicycle."

JB and Annie moved from Staten Island to Van Dyke Street, Brooklyn, near the Schuyler, Payne & Caddell Yard, in 1903. In 1906 they moved to a house at 85th Street and Shore Road in the Bay Ridge section of Brooklyn. Young Leroy grew up there and attended P.S. 118 and Manual Training High School. Later his parents sent him to the Hallock School in Great Barrington, Massachusetts, from which he graduated in 1914.

Leroy was tall and handsome, a lover of dancing, fine food, and elegant clothes, and he spread his wings while away from home for the first time at Hallock. Many of JB's letters to him read like this one:

I have just received a bill—$15—dancing lessons. ...your expenses are increasing all the time. You must be more saving. Answer at once and tell me how you are. Guess I had better bring you home and put you to work in the yard.

Love, Papa

Leroy's sister Lillian was the oldest, and after Leroy came Laura, Beatrice, and Marjean. Because he was the only boy in the family, it was understood that Leroy would follow in the footsteps of his father and uncles and choose a career in the maritime industry. He attended Princeton University for a year, but in 1917, as the country entered World War I, he dropped out and enlisted in the Navy.

Leroy served for a year as Second Assistant Engineer on the privately-owned motor yacht, the *Tarantula*, which was stationed in Brooklyn. Her captain, William K.

The motor yacht *Tarantula* prior to World War I.

PHOTO: Collection of the U.S. Naval Historical Center

Vanderbilt, was the son of Commodore Cornelius Vanderbilt, who had been, among other things, a successful ferry operator in New York Harbor. William volunteered the *Tarantula* for coastal patrols looking for enemy U-boats off shore. The crew, Leroy recalled, fished off the yacht by day and spent the evenings at the St. George Hotel in Brooklyn.

After a year, the Navy sent Leroy to the Baylies Shipyard in Port Jefferson, Long Island. He took charge of building two 250-foot long naval battle practice targets made of wood. They had a six-foot draft, with massive hemlock beams fastened crossways and down, and thirty masts that each rose forty feet above the waterline. Navy destroyers towed them out to sea, and pilots in training used them for target practice. Leroy put what he had witnessed in the shipyard as a boy to good use.

Discharged in May 1919, he enrolled in Ulmark's Nautical School and Packard Commercial School in Manhattan and studied at Pratt School of Engineering in Brooklyn. When he officially joined the yard staff, he took on greater responsibilities for his father and installed the first double-entry bookkeeping system for its financial records. Although he always retained certain traditional touches in his style, Leroy assumed the responsibility of bringing Caddell's into the twentieth century.

These were perhaps the most colorful years at Caddell's, with Leroy at the helm and an array of extraordinary customers coming through his door. As president, he ran the company like a private club. The Blue Room, which faced Richmond Terrace, served as the bar room and company restaurant, the place where management and customers socialized. The yard lunchroom was on Richmond Terrace, and on weekday mornings, Clara, the cook, or Rose, her successor, would serve breakfast at six and lunch at 11:30. The yard also had a game room with shuffleboard. In the evenings, Leroy, his family, and friends frequented the Meurot Club in St. George and the Villa Restaurant in Stapleton.

Two views of the rum runner *Marshall McCoy* in dry dock at the John B. Caddell Dry Dock Company's new Staten Island yard, c. 1916
PHOTOS: Collection of Caddell Dry Dock and Repair Company

During Prohibition, the rumrunner *Marshall McCoy* came into the yard from time to time for repairs. Her captain was a notorious pirate who always paid either in cash or in rum—or both. Captain McCoy would tie up at night, and Leroy would make sure the repairs he needed were completed in time for him to leave under cover of darkness. Often when McCoy and other bootleggers came to the yard for repairs, they shared the facility with their arch-enemy, the U.S. Coast Guard. A Coast Guard cutter might well be on one dry dock, and the bootlegger's boat on another—at the opposite end of the yard. Leroy would see that the two never met.

He was respected for his toughness, but like JB, Leroy had a generous heart. Employees were like family. As his father had, he loaned money to them so they could buy homes, and like his father, Leroy asked only for a handshake and an IOU. When one of his favorite restaurants, the Villa, was about to go out of business, in his usual style he loaned the owner the money needed to keep the place afloat.

On the other hand, if he did not like you, Leroy would not do business with you, and it was not uncommon for him to turn away a disagreeable customer. Under Leroy's management of the shipyard, coastal schooners, small excursion boats, ferries, deep-sea fishing boats and yachts joined the ranks of Harbor craft customers, like tugs, motor tankers, and barges. His customers were often "characters," his son recalled years later. Nonetheless, "business relationships were generous, with people whose moral fiber was 100 percent. A handshake was worth a thousand lawyers' papers."

The business continued to prosper through the Great Depression of the 1930s. Oil transportation thrived in the harbor, and among Caddell's best customers were Socony and Esso. Berwind Coal was a mainstay, as was Tracy Towing, and Leroy quietly built a large customer base on their business.

In spite of the economic hardships the country was experiencing, Caddell's expanded during the Great Depression of the 1930s, and in 1936 Leroy bought the Larsen Shipyard to the west of his yard.

The Berwind White steam tugboat *Edward J. Berwind* and a steel coal barge, c. 1930

PHOTO: Collection of Caddell Dry Dock and Repair Company

The *Staten Island Advance* marveled that the sale was "one of the biggest transactions of its kind in the borough since United Shipyards bought out the old Sisco works in 1927." Leroy incorporated Larsen's and converted dry dock #2 from steam to electricity. The acquisition also gave him one more pier and one more dry dock, #3, which was 151 feet in length overall, with 121 feet of "box" and two 17-foot "aprons," or outriggers, off each end of the box.

But by 1937 the labor unrest which plagued many industries in the United States throughout the 1930s came into the yard. That same year, 75 wood caulkers finished removing all the caulking from the bottom seams of a large coastal schooner lying in dry dock #2, walked off the job, and declared a strike for a pay increase. They had abandoned the ship when she was only partially repaired and still in dry dock, but Leroy was unbowed. He hired

(continued on page 27)

Dated February 29, 1928, this photograph of Caddell's Staten Island yard taken from the wing wall of dry dock #2 features, *from the left*, a Carrol Towing Company tug, a yard tug, a stick lighter; a floating derrick, and another yard tug.

PHOTO: Collection of Caddell Dry Dock and Repair Company

A Reliable Fuel Company tanker on dry dock #3 in 1935; Chester A. Poling and Harold Tabeling owned the company.

PHOTO: Collection of Caddell Dry Dock and Repair Company

Damage and repair, c. 1930

The barge *Eureka*, owned by the Berwind White Coal Company, on dry dock #3. The series shows the damage to the barge, *above*, and the completed repairs, *facing page*. Caddell's rebuilt her after she was hit by a tug and her hull was smashed.

In addition to repairing them, Caddell's also built coal barges for Berwind White.

PHOTOS: Collection of Caddell Dry Dock and Repair Company

The motor tanker *John B. Caddell*

Above: The launching of the *John B. Caddell* took place in 1938. JB is at the center of the photograph, Mrs. Carol Poling is to his right, and to his left, holding the bouquet, is the ship's sponsor, JB's wife Annie. Chester Poling started fueling yachts in New York Harbor in the 1920s, and Caddell's did repairs and installed new tanks in his wooden tanker. JB, and later Leroy, helped finance Poling's company as he expanded his fleet, and by the early 1940s, Poling Transportation Company was strong financially and had repaid all the mortgages it owed to the Caddells. In gratitude for his support, Chester built and launched the *John B. Caddell* to deliver oil products to terminals from New York to Boston. The Navy commandeered and used her to fuel warships and terminals during World War II. The shipyard continued to repair Poling's ships, which Chester, and his brother and company co-owner, Robert, ran until the 1990s. Janet, Robert's daughter, operated the company briefly, liquidated the assets, and retired. Chester and Robert's grand-nephew Edwin and Gary Cutler bought four vessels, including the *John B. Caddell*, from her and started Poling and Cutler Marine Transportation in 1995.

PHOTO: Collection of Caddell Dry Dock and Repair Company

The Company & Its History

Above: The *John B. Caddell*, 1988.
PHOTO: Daniel Hormann

Left: The *John B. Caddell* in dry dock #1 in 2002.
PHOTO: Steve Kalil, Collection of Caddell Dry Dock and Repair Company

The Breezy Point Ferry in dry dock, c. 1935

The Breezy Point Ferry service, owned by Frank Clair, dates back to the 1920s. The boats ferried summer vacationers from Sheepshead Bay to Breezy Point, Long Island through the 1980s. Pictured here are the *Frederick Lundy*, top, and the *Washington Coyler* in dry dock. Clair was also a shareholder, along with Frank Barry and Jerry Driscoll, in the Circle Line, the famous sightseeing boats that circumnavigate Manhattan Island. The Statue of Liberty Line now owns the operation.

In addition to repairing the Staten Island ferries, Caddell's works on the Port Jefferson ferries, New York Waterways ferries, the Statue of Liberty Line boats, and the Governor's Island ferry.

PHOTOS: Collection of Caddell Dry Dock and Repair Company

The Company & Its History

A coal collier in dry dock #4, 1948

The coal collier pictured here is a "dead" ship. She had to be towed to the shipyard because her machinery had been taken out, and she had been converted from a self-propelled ship into a barge.

Leroy purchased dry dock #4 from the government after World War II. Built in 1945 for the U.S. Navy to haul destroyer escorts, it had never been used and was lying in Quanset, Rhode Island.

PHOTOS: Collection of Caddell Dry Dock and Repair Company

Caddell Dry Dock: 100 Years Harborside

Damage and repair to the *Esso Tug No. 11*, 1953

Left: Sideswiped by the ship she was approaching to escort into the Harbor, the *Esso Tug No. 11*'s wheelhouse was badly mangled. Among the many dangers tugs face, the moment when one closes in on a huge ship, a massive wall of steel rising out of the water, is the most dangerous. Rubber fenders protect the tug's hull, but once its lines are attached to a ship, the immense force of the ship pulling the hawser could cause the tug to list toward it, and be damaged or sink.

Above: Esso Tug No. 11 in dry dock with repairs complete, September 11, 1953.

PHOTOS: Collection of Caddell Dry Dock and Repair Company

Tug repair

Above: The steam tug *M. & J. Tracy*, launched in 1919 in New Orleans, Louisiana by the W.J. Tracy Towing Line, in dry dock. In 1956, McAllister Towing and Transportation Company purchased her and renamed her the *Patrice McAllister*. McAllister converted her from steam to diesel-powered engines in 1957, and she worked for the company until October 4, 1976, when she sank off the New Jersey coast near Atlantic City as she was going from Camden to the McAllister shipyard in Jersey City, New Jersey.

Right: The steam tug *Anne Moran*, launched in 1938 in Bay City, Michigan, in dry dock, April, 1973. She sank on April 10, 1976.

PHOTOS: Collection of Caddell Dry Dock and Repair Company

caulkers from out of state to finish the job and sent the ship to the Perth Amboy Dry Dock to complete the rest of the repair. Months later he settled the strike with a small pay increase—pennies in comparison to what the strikers had demanded. He had held his ground, and his colleagues in the industry respected him for it. They had supported Caddell's throughout the strike and helped him keep the yard going.

As World War II approached, Caddell's was exceptionally busy; New York Harbor was bustling with warships and commercial vessels. In the midst of this prosperity and activity, Leroy married Ruth Nordenholt, a Staten Island girl, at Judge Ernest Smith's house on Emerson Hill in Staten Island in 1940. They rented an apartment on Hart Boulevard on Staten Island, and later bought a home in Colonia, New Jersey, they dubbed "The Five

At the Meurot Club

The Meurot Club in St. George was a favorite watering hole for Caddell's managers and customers. Pictured here around 1945 are a number of staff members from the Tracy Towing Company, including Jim Heany, the office manager, standing at the left, and Bill Lane, a shore captain for Tracy's, seated at the left. Leroy Caddell is sitting second from the left at the checkered table. Many deals were struck with a handshake over a drink here, at the old Villa Restaurant in Stapleton, and at the Blue Room, the yard dining room.

PHOTO: Collection of Caddell Dry Dock and Repair Company

Three generations of Caddells; *from left to right*, JBC, age 5, Leroy, and JB
PHOTO: Collection of John B. Caddell II

Chimneys." In 1944 they moved from Colonia back to Staten Island to 8 Buttonwood Road in Dongan Hills, to be closer to friends, the shipyard, and the Richmond County Country Club, where Leroy loved to play golf.

In 1951, JB passed away. He had continued to make trips, alone, to Maple Grove in Nova Scotia to visit the family farm and support the small community. Among his many charitable acts was his donation of funds to build a school. Ever sentimental, he loved his old home, kept the farmhouse, and remained reluctant to allow anyone to move into it.

On one of his last trips, he inspired a poem. Eva Mae Potts had a friend in Noel, Nova Scotia who told her how, as Eva wrote to JB in 1949, "…in your childhood you loved the old hearthstone which you played around in your parents' home. Then she told me how after many years you returned, finding the old house had sunken into the ground, and all that was left was the old hearthstone… She said you sat right down and put your feet on it."

Here are a few stanzas from her poem, "The Old Hearthstone."

I place my feet on the old hearthstone,
It brings sweet dreams of the dear old home,
Of a mother's love and tender care
And where we once all knelt in prayer.
In boyhood there in strength I grew
And many happy years I knew,
Within that humble, loving home
Around the glow of the old hearthstone…

Long years ago with my feet there
I heard a mother's fervent prayer
That would guide me where I'd roam
And had to leave the old hearthstone.
A millionaire I am today—
A prosperous man in every way;
Now living in my palace home
I have my dreams of the old hearthstone.

This word is to mothers everywhere;
Hold up your boy in faith and prayer—
For all your griefs he will atone
And live to bless the old hearthstone.

Eva Mae Potts

An aerial view of Caddell Dry Dock and Repair Co., c. 1947

From left: The Poling Transportation yard property; Vanbro Sand & Gravel Company, with its small finger pier; Caddell's boiler house, where they housed the compressors and manufactured steam for the dry dock pumps. Note the space between the boiler house and the next building, the carpenter's shop/mill. It was left for the bowsprits of sailing ships. The boiler house was destroyed by fire in 1975, and most of the yard's patterns were lost.

At Pier #1, a Hudson River Line excursion boat is tied up. A stick lighter is on dry dock #1.

The fishing boat *Glory*, owned by Captain Jacob Martin, is alongside the Berwind White tug *Admiral Dewey*, and two Tracy tugs. All three steam tugs are tied up to the main bulkhead east of Pier 2, along with the yard's two tugs, the *Jay Bee* and the *Jay Bee II*.

On dry dock #4 is an Esso motor tanker built in the 1920s for the Standard Oil Company.

Lying on the Caddell pier heads of Piers 2 and 3 are three barges, a steel coal barge that was converted to carry oil, a steel coal barge, and a wooden coal barge.

A steel coal barge owned either by Tracy or Berwind is on dry dock #3. To its left is the General Contracting Company's floating derrick. In the background the Markham Homes are under construction. Quinlan Oil owns the coal silos in the lower left. They are still standing today.

PHOTO: Collection of Caddell Dry Dock and Repair Company

Like his grandfather and father, John Bartlett Caddell II, Leroy's son, was the only boy in a family of girls. He attended high school away from home at the Lawrenceville School in New Jersey and college at the University of Miami. But he eagerly awaited summer vacations, when he could roam his father's fascinating shipyard, where Claude Forbes took him under his wing. He was dubbed "JBC."

JBC asserted that Claude "…was one of the brightest guys I ever met in my life. Of everyone in the whole yard, he was an encyclopedia of the shipyard business. He did everything. He ran the cranes, and he ran the boats. He made sure everything was working. Of course he had his own little cubbyholes where he put things. If you wanted anything in the shipyard and you couldn't find it, you went to Claude."

Young John's sensibilities are in some ways more like those of his great-uncles than those of his grandfather, who was, as he commented, "not sea friendly" and subject to sea sickness. Unlike him, as a boy John loved boats, sailing, and the sea as much as he loved the hum of the shipyard. His father quickly recognized these traits, and when John graduated from college in 1966, Leroy passed the reins of the daily operations over to him and made him the president of the company.

Leroy remained as Chairman and CEO and spent the summer months on Staten Island, but, as his father had done, he wintered in Florida. As much as JBC would have preferred to run Caddell's in the style of

Claude Forbes and John B. Caddell II, 2004; Claude took his first job at the yard for a wage of $.37 per hour in 1931 and worked at Caddell's for 72 years. PHOTO: Michael Falco

his grandfather and father, with its club atmosphere and family feel, he saw that the industry was changing, transforming from the days of the handshake to days of red tape. He hired Ralph Merrill, a close friend and customer, as General Manager in 1967. Before coming aboard, Merrill had wrestled with the New York City bureaucracy as Marine Supervisor for the Department of Sanitation and later as Director of Ferry Operations for the Staten Island Ferry. "He wasn't anything but brilliant when it came to the maritime business," JBC recalled. "He did a wonderful job for us."

Increasing government scrutiny of the business continued to prove extremely costly and time-consuming. "I think we have to live in a world of laws and regulations. I have no problem with that," JBC remarked recently, about the paperwork that now governs the world of shipping. "It's just that everything's been duplicated and quadruplicated. You just get finished with one, and another envelops that, so, in effect, the regulations are keeping people from being able to function."

Merrill's 23-year tenure helped JBC deal with the "ungodly regulations" that beleaguered his business, and in spite of the difficulties, JBC managed in 1972 to purchase the Brewer Dry Dock Company yard. Originally the Brighton Marine Shipyard, it had been owned by the Delaware & Lakawanna Railroad, which had closed it and sold it to Brewer's. Ferry service from New York City to Hoboken and Jersey City had ended in the late 1960s, and the railroad no longer needed the facility to repair its railroad car floats, tugboats, and ferries.

JBC had his eye on the property, but Brewer's managed to buy it first. They ran it for a couple of years and generally mishandled the facility. When they were ready to give it up, JBC was ready to buy it, in spite of its condition. Brewer's dry dock #1 was badly burned, and dry dock #2 had sunk. JBC repaired and modernized dry dock #1, raised dry dock

Leroy Willis Caddell, 1976
PHOTO: Collection of John B. Caddell II

#2 and towed it, along with dry docks #3 and #4, out to sea for disposal. He also repaired and installed new pumps in dry dock #5. Little by little JBC established the East Yard, where, in 1979, he built a tank-cleaning plant, and a steam-generating facility used to clean barges, tankers and other vessels.

Meanwhile, disaster struck the thriving shipyard. A disgruntled employee set fire to Caddell's boiler and compressor building, and JBC saw the destruction of much of the yard's history. All of Wentworth Forbes' patterns for ship's parts were destroyed, as were most of the carpenters' tools, and the building.

But the sensibility of the yard endured, and that spirit is described warmly in a letter written in October of 1968 to Leroy from the captain of the motor vessel *Glory*, a 120-foot head boat out of Sheepshead Bay, Brooklyn, that ran daily fishing charters. Over the years it often came to Caddell's for repairs. "Mrs. Martin and I wish to thank you, Young John, and Ray for your very nice letter of congratulations and the gifts of champagne, on our 59th anniversary," Captain Jacob Martin wrote. "Coming from such nice folks as you have been for so many years, it sure made us happy and, like you mention, it will give us the spirit to carry on."

An important newcomer arrived on the scene in 1975, when Steven Kalil, a young carpenter, joined the staff as a carpenter's helper. Kalil's rise in the firm is a story characteristic of a family firm like Caddell's. He recalls that his first task was building his own toolbox, a tradition from the days of JB. After he had worked at the yard for a year, JBC recognized his interest in ship repair and his potential for management and invited him to work under Ralph Merrill in the office. Kalil accepted, Merrill taught him how to manage the yard, and gradually he took over the responsibilities of its day-to-day operations. In 1987 Leroy passed away, and in 1988, Merrill retired.

In the summer of 1989, JBC invited the staff to the launching of his new yacht *Yorel* in Maine. He had commissioned Hodgdon Yachts, Inc., boat builders in East Boothbay Harbor, and by doing so, revitalized the dying business. The Hodgdon staff increased from eight to 50 employees, and today the company has grown even larger and builds modern wooden boats. JBC gave the shipbuilder new life, and his ancestors would have been proud.

In behavior uncharacteristic of a very private man, JBC surprised the crowd with his very public announcement naming Steve Kalil president of the company.

As the rest of the shipyards of the Harbor went out of business, JBC was able to expand his, largely because of its reputation and his willingness to work with customers and make adjustments according to the changes in the industry. He saw, for example, that his customers were expanding the size of their vessels, and they needed larger dry docks. In 1986 he purchased dry dock #6 from a developer in Baltimore who was planning to convert the old Bethlehem Key Highway Shipyard to condominiums. It is the yard's largest dry dock, measuring 400 feet long by 115 feet wide at the base.

Caddell's repairs the Staten Island Ferry fleet, and tugs, tankers, lighters, and barges from all of the major marine transport companies on the East Coast of the United States, including Bouchard Transportation, Buchanan Marine, Donjon Marine, K-Sea Transportation, McAllister Towing and Transportation, Moran Towing and Transportation, Penn Maritime, Reinauer Transportation, and Weeks Marine.

Because he has kept the yard active, JBC has been able to upgrade it regularly. He shored up his holdings along the Kill van

Kull by purchasing two properties to the east of the main yard, the Poling Transportation property in 1985 and the Standard Boat property in 1990. In 1989 he also disposed of old dry dock #3 by sinking it for a fishing reef off Fire Island and replacing it with a steel dock of similar capacity and size from a shipyard in Rockland, Maine. In 1999 he commissioned dry dock #7, a large tug dock, 160 feet long by 80 feet wide overall with a height of 43 feet.

In 2002 he donated dry dock #2, built by his grandfather, to the North River Tugboat Museum and replaced it with a new, larger, steel dry dock #2, built in Texas and purchased from the Rhode Island-based firm, American Shipyards.

In 2006, a wing wall on dry dock #4, a wooden Navy dock, collapsed, and the dock sank. JBC had it dug out and removed, and purchased a new dry dock #4 through marine broker Hughes Brothers. The new #4 dry dock, coincidentally, had also been built in 1942 for the Navy but it had not seen World War II service. After the war the Navy sold it to the Coast Guard, which used it at its Baltimore, Maryland base.

In the same year, 2006, JBC commissioned the construction of a steel dry dock #8, specifically designed to repair large tugboats. It measures 160 by 90 feet and is 39 feet high, or about half the length of a football field and as high as a five-story building. Capable of handling 10,000 horsepower tugs weighing as much as 2,000 tons, it can raise a boat in an hour, a

"JBC," John B. Caddell II, 2003
PHOTO: Collection of Caddell Dry Dock and Repair Company

factor that allows workers to make repairs and get the tug back into service quickly.

The purchase represents Caddell's response to changes in the maritime industry over that 60-year period. Because barges, particularly petroleum barges, have become bigger, the tugs that handle them have become bigger. The new steel dry dock is the only floating dry dock in the New York metropolitan area that can handle such massive vessels.

Steve Kalil, named president of the company in 1989, atop the wing wall of dry dock #1. PHOTO: Michael Falco

Over the last quarter of the twentieth century, Caddell's has gained distinction for its willingness to work with not-for-profit organizations that take care of historic vessels. In 1985, JBC put the historic Portuguese bark *The Gazela of Philadelphia* on dry dock. JBC allowed volunteers to work on recaulking and sheeting the ship's hull with copper free of charge.

The famous replica of Henry Hudson's *Half Moon*, the first European vessel to sail into New York Harbor on its way up the Hudson River, has come to Caddell's for repair work several times, as have South Street Seaport Museum's three historic ships, the lightship *Ambrose*, and the tall ships *Peking* and *Wavertree*.

In 1987 Caddell's hauled out the *Peking* to repair her steel hull, and sandblast and paint her. In 1999, South Street Seaport Museum contracted the shipyard to dry dock the *Wavertree*, for hull repairs and to build yards for her. In response to this unusual and challenging task, Kalil called then 69-year old Artie Elams out of retirement to make them. Made of conical shapes that fit together and are tapered at the ends, one yard is 80 feet long, and the other is 90 feet long. Each massive yard weighs several tons.

This attention to history is important to JBC as he continually wrestles with less rewarding aspects of the modern marine industry. The hand of government regulation has afflicted the shipyard since he took over in the 1960s. "Somebody is going to realize that moving things by water causes much less pollution than moving things on land," Steve Kalil commented. "Nobody seems concerned about moving things by truck, even though it's ten to fifteen times more polluting than moving something by ship or barge."

Government regulations, based often on alarmist environmentalist notions, have taken their toll on the expenses of

(continued on page 46)

Damage to the *Elizabeth Moran*, 1987

Joseph Borst, dockmaster, stands with the tug. Hit by the bulbous bow of a large tanker while coming into New York Harbor in fog, the tug would have sunk immediately, but the tanker's bow remained imbedded in the hull of the tug, keeping her from sinking and allowing the crew time to escape. In the process of repair, Caddell's removed the damaged portion of the tug and rigged out its two main engines.

PHOTOS: Collection of Caddell Dry Dock and Repair Company

The *Gazela of Philadelphia* in dry dock, 1986

The Portuguese Grand Banks fishing vessel, the square-rigged barquentine *Gazela Primeiro* was built in the shipyard of J. M. Mendes in Setubal, Portugal in 1901. With a crew of 40, she set sail from Lisbon for the Grand Banks and could stow up to 350 tons of cod packed in salt in her hold. She made her last commercial trip in 1969 and was laid up until word reached the Philadelphia Maritime Museum that she was available, and philanthropist William Wikoff Smith purchased her for the museum. In 1971, she sailed for Philadelphia, tracing Columbus' route via the Canary Islands and San Juan, Puerto Rico. The Philadelphia Ship Preservation Guild took over her operation in 1985 and renamed her the *Gazela of Philadelphia*. She became the maritime ambassador for the City of Philadelphia and the Commonwealth of Pennsylvania and has participated in many domestic and international events, including *OpSail 2000*. She is pictured here in dry dock in March, 1986.

PHOTO: Steve Kalil, Collection of Caddell Dry Dock and Repair Company

The *Peking* in dry dock, 1987

Left: The 347-foot four-masted barque *Peking* was built in Germany in 1911 as one of the famous Flying P line of square riggers serving in the Cape Horn trade to Chile. She is the second largest surviving Cape Horner in the world. She made a career transporting general cargo from Europe to South America and returning with nitrates to fertilize the fields of Europe. After the nitrate trade collapsed, she was sold in 1932 to Shaftesbury Homes, a British charity for children, renamed *Arethusa*, and used as a stationary school ship. The Aron Foundation bought her in 1974, and after an extensive refit, she was towed across the Atlantic to South Street Seaport Museum, where her restoration continues, and she is moored at Pier 16. She is pictured here in dry dock #6 in June, 1987.

Right: The yard tug *JB V* shifts her off dry dock #6, 1987.

PHOTOS: *Left*: Steve Kalil, *Right*: Barry Masterson, Collection of Caddell Dry Dock and Repair Company

Caddell Dry Dock: 100 Years Harborside

The Coast Guard cutter *Eagle*, known as America's Tall Ship, in dry dock, 1989

The vessel that became the U.S. Coast Guard's good will ambassador ship was launched in Hamburg, Germany in 1936 as the *Horst Wessel*, and first served as a training ship for the German Navy under Hitler's Third Reich. She ended the war grounded at the German port of Bremerhaven. Awarded to the United States as reparation after the war, she was recommissioned as *USCG Eagle* and sailed to her new home at the U.S. Coast Guard Academy in New London, Connecticut in 1947; the cooperation of the veteran German and young Coast Guard crews pulling together during the trip got her through a North Atlantic hurricane. Since then she has logged thousands of miles training future Coast Guard officers in the disciplines of seafaring.

PHOTO: Steve Kalil, Collection of Caddell Dry Dock and Repair Company

The *HMS Rose* in dry dock, 1989

Dry docked at Caddell's in March, 1989, *HMS Rose* is a replica of an 18th century Royal Navy frigate that cruised the American coast during the Revolutionary War. Built in Lunenburg, Nova Scotia, the *Rose* operated as a sail training vessel from 1985 to 2001. In 2003 the ship appeared as *HMS Surprise* in the 20th Century Fox film *Master and Commander: The Far Side of the World* directed by Peter Weir. Now renamed *Surprise* in honor of her role in the film, the ship is open to the public daily at the Maritime Museum of San Diego.

PHOTOS: Barry Masterson, Collection of Caddell Dry Dock and Repair Company

The tall ship *Wavertree* in dry dock #6, 2000

Built as a cargo vessel at Southhampton, England in 1885 for R.W. Leyland & Company of Liverpool, the *Wavertree* is one of the last large sailing ships built of wrought iron. Her first cargo was jute transported between India and Scotland, but with less then two years under sail, she entered the tramp trade, taking cargoes anywhere in the world. She sailed for a quarter century, until she was dismasted off Cape Horn in 1910. First used in Chile as a warehouse, she was converted into a sand barge in Argentina in 1947. In 1968 South Street Seaport Museum acquired her and is restoring her as a sailing vessel.

Left: Caddell's replaced two yards the *Wavertree* lost off Cape Horn in 1910; one 80 and the other 90 feet long. Each weighs several tons.

PHOTOS: *Top*: Francis J. Duffy, *Left*: Steve Kalil, Collection of Caddell Dry Dock and Repair Company

The Company & Its History

The double-hull oil tanker barge, the *Bouchard B. No. 242* in dry dock #6, 2007

The 80 feet wide by 467 feet long barge carries 138,000 barrels, or 5,796,000 gallons of petroleum or the equivalent of 2,070 tractor trailer truckloads of fuel. The use of marine transport is ecologically sound and helps take millions of polluting, road damaging, traffic-clogging trucks off the highways.

PHOTOS: Steve Kalil, Collection of Caddell Dry Dock and Repair Company

Caddell Dry Dock: 100 Years Harborside

Staten Island Ferries in dry dock

Staten Island ferries make 110 five-mile trips daily from St. George, Staten Island to the Whitehall Terminal at the tip of lower Manhattan. Caddell's has been servicing them since 1986, when the company bought dry dock #6.

Above and left: The Staten Island ferry *Andrew J. Barberi*, built in 1981, is 310 feet long, 70 feet wide, and has a draft of 13½ feet. The 7,000 horsepower ferry weighs 3,335 gross tons and carries 6,000 passengers. Caddell's rebuilt the *Barberi* after it struck the ferry maintenance pier on October 15, 2003. The pier structure tore through the ferry's main deck, injured 71 people and killed eleven. The part of the ferry that was damaged in the allision, as such maritime accidents are termed, has been repaired but has not yet been repainted in these photographs.

The Company & Its History

Above: Built in 1986, the *John A. Noble* is pictured in dry dock in 1989. It is one of two *Austen* class boats, small commuter ferries that are used for night and weekend runs that carry 1,300 passengers. The 3,200 horsepower *Alice Austen* and *Noble* ferries, named for two Staten Island artists, are 207 feet long, 40 feet wide, and have a draft of 8½ feet; each weighs 499 tons, or about one quarter of the weight of the *Barberi* class boats.

Right: Caddell's also repairs *Kennedy* class ferries, which carry 3,500 passengers, and the *Molinari* class ferries launched in 2004 and 2005. Although similar in length and width to the *Barberi* class ferries, the *Guy V. Molinari*, along with the *Sen. John J. Marchi* and the *Spirit of America*, are the largest in the Staten Island ferry fleet. They have an additional vehicle deck that accommodates 40 automobiles, and they can transport 4,400 people.

PHOTOS: Steve Kalil, Collection of Caddell Dry Dock and Repair Company

The *Big Betty*, named for JBC's sister, Betty Clements, is one of four floating cranes at the shipyard. Purchased from Weeks Marine in 1990, she has a lifting capacity of 50 tons and a boom length of over 210 feet. She primarily services dry dock #6, Caddell's largest dry dock, by supplying shipyard workers with the equipment, machinery, and materials they use.

PHOTO: Michael Falco

Dry dock #1, built in 1916, is one of the last floating wood dry docks in operation in the world. Constructed out of long leaf yellow pine, it was designed to accommodate the Erie Lackawana Railroad's passenger and car ferries that ran from Hoboken and Jersey City to Manhattan. The dry dock's well-preserved box is original and as durable as the day it was built. Its original pumping system was located on one wing wall and powered by a 200 horsepower electric motor driving numerous "deep wells" by a common shaft. The shaft attached to each of the deep wells shafts that ran the full length of the dry dock on top of its wing wall and activated the pumps as it rotated.

In the late 1970s, Caddell's rebuilt the dry dock's wing walls with Oregon pine and modernized its pumping system by installing individual electric pumps for each watertight compartment. This made the hauling out and undocking processes much simpler and more easily controlled by the dockmaster. Caddell's has not retired dry dock #1 and replaced it with a steel dry dock because it remains strong. Nonetheless it requires costly and time-consuming maintenance, including wedging and caulking the many thousands of feet of box, deck and wing wall plank seams, and its useful life is drawing to a close. The Harbor lacks knowledgeable and qualified shipwrights and wood caulkers, lost trades in New York, to maintain it. Nonetheless, as long as John B. Caddell runs Caddell's, this living memorial to history and his father and grandfather may well be worth the effort to locate and train such workers.

PHOTO: Michael Falco

operating a small firm like Caddell's. "Someone has pushed this pendulum so far in one direction that they're shutting businesses down," Kalil said.

JBC underscores that sentiment: "Over-regulation is a real negative to our industry. It is the most important cause of the loss of so many shipyards."

Kalil has seen the Harbor become dominated with fewer but much larger vessels, the immense containerships, and the trucks that service them. For a yard that deals in harborcraft like barges and tugs, that trend led to a financial decline in the 1980s. The decline stabilized by 2000, as more and more people began rediscovering that it is much cheaper, faster, and cleaner to move goods on the water than on the land. Because of this reawakening, there has been a steady increase in business and the number of support vessels that the industry requires.

As other shipyards have closed, Caddell's has picked up their talent and their business. JBC has kept the yard going and well maintained even in difficult times. The yard's growth has been cautious and intelligent, often because he has not been tempted to gear up for large government contracts only to be forced, in turn, to downsize for commercial work. Rather he has opted to specialize in harbor and coastal craft.

JBC has maintained his forefathers' management style. He respects his employees and expects the best from them. They respond with energy, and disciplined, highly-skilled efforts. He has set the pay scale at his yard well above union scale and fights what he considers to be a crippling, enervating union requirement known as "strict classification." He believes that set of rules—specifying that a certain job can be carried out only by a worker specified in that job classification—killed the rest of the yards in the Harbor. At his yard, he capitalizes on the broad range of talents natural to the people who work there instead of hiring a specialist for each task. Workers interface on many aspects of repair and operations and often cross lines and perform tasks that would be limited to one person in a union yard. Many of them are skilled at a variety of distinct tasks, like iron working, mechanics, electrical work, carpentry, rigging, and welding, and they are paid accordingly. The practice has added vitality and accomplished expertise to the components of JBC's successful shipyard.

JBC's persistence, coupled with his inbred trust in the natural ebb and flow of industry, is paying off. Since 1961, when he took over and carried on the work of his father and his grandfather, over thirty shipyards in the harbor have closed. But since the turn of the new century, people have begun to rediscover the economic and environmental advantages of water transport. As he commented recently, "Our customers don't want us to go out of business. We are one of the last legitimate shipyards." And, as New York Harbor finds itself in a battle with other major American ports to maintain its dominance, its maritime businesses are struggling to reestablish piers, transport routes, and harbor facilities, stripped away in a misguided effort to rob the Port of its industry and replace it with retail businesses, recreational facilities, and housing.

Through it all, Caddell's high standards—forged by JB, Leroy and John B. Caddell II—have kept the company alive. To accommodate them, and the resurgence in the maritime industry, he has expanded the yard and its capabilities, and done it while upholding the Caddell trademark—efficient, expert ship repair. Caddell's is the oldest, largest, and busiest shipyard left in New York. Over one hundred years of service, renowned for fairness and enduring craftsmanship, has made the company a mainstay of New York Harbor and one of the peerless leaders of the maritime industry in America.

Built especially for high horsepower tugboats, dry dock #8 was built on Staten Island at May Ship Repair Contracting Corporation in Mariner's Harbor in 2006 and put into service in 2007. *Above:* The yard tug *LW Caddell* is maneuvering it from the repair berth, where it was outfitted, to a working berth in Caddell's main yard, where it will begin operation.

PHOTO: Steve Kalil, Collection of Caddell Dry Dock and Repair Company

Dry Docking

Previous page: Dry dock #7 with a Moran tug in the background.
PHOTO: Michael Falco

Dry Docking

The Statue of Liberty Line ferry *Miss New Jersey* in dry dock #1, 2007.
PHOTO: Michael Falco

Dry docking, the process of getting a ship out of the water to clean and make repairs below the waterline, began in ancient times when mariners brought their vessels ashore at high tide, heeled them over, made repairs, and "breamed" the hull before the tide re-floated them. This process, "laying a ship aground," or "careening," is still used today, but mostly with small boats in areas where there is a strong tidal range. Workers ground the vessel on a slope and pull it over or secure it with blocks and tackles from the mast to a fixed object. Depending on the contour of the hull and the weight and size of the craft, they can slowly ease it onto the beach.

Breaming is the process by which workers burn off the accumulated growth on a wooden ship's hull and then pave her with tar. As the tide comes in, they turn the ship over, lay her aground on the tarred side, and repeat the process on the other side.

Todd Shipyard's graving dock in Erie Basin became the largest graving dock on the Atlantic seaboard when it was rebuilt in steel and concrete and reopened in 1928. Originally constructed of timber in 1881, Todd's expanded it to 750 feet in length, with a width at the top of the keel blocks of 90 feet and a top width of 120 feet. The full dock, which could contain more than 15,000,000 gallons of water, had both an outer and an inner gate seal and could accommodate two vessels at one time. In 2007, in spite of the maritime industry's burgeoning needs, the graving dry dock was filled in and the area paved over for a parking lot.   PHOTO: Courtesy of the Brooklyn Historical Society

Over time, laying ships aground gradually gave way to "graving" them. The term *to grave* could possibly be derived from the French word *grève*, or shore. The first stone dry docks were tidally based and had no mechanical means with which to pump out water, so workers could work on the vessel only at low tide. As the tide went out, the ship's hull came to rest on keel blocks. Then riggers used bracing poles, or spur shores, and rope to keep it upright. The obvious advantage of the permanent dry dock is that it allows workers to access hulls from all sides at once and complete repairs and cleaning in a much more efficient manner.

According to the ancient Greek author Athenaeus of Naucratis, the first dry dock was invented in Ptolemaic Egypt sometime after 204 B.C., when a Phoenician mariner devised what is now known as a graving

The deck of Caddell's floating dry dock #7, showing the keel blocks, bilge blocks, and wing walls.
PHOTO: Michael Falco

dock. This unknown maritime engineer instructed his workers to dig a trench close to the shore and in it build stone bases across which they could lay beams crosswise running the length and width of the trench. To fill the trench with water, he had them dig a channel from the sea and float the ship down it into the trench. Once the ship had been secured, workers could close the entrance to the trench, pump off the water, and slowly rest the vessel on the crossbeams so that they could overhaul it.

Similar dry docks had appeared in China by 1079 A.D. The Song Dynasty scientist Shen Kuo describes how a palace official suggested excavating a wide, basin-like trench at the end of Beijing's Chin-ming Lake and filling it with water to serve as a graving dock for two huge "dragon ships" that had been presented to the throne as

(continued on page 56)

The wing wall of dry dock #7

Clockwise from left: A wing wall with pull chains, pulleys, and the gauge board or "fingerboard." The flood gates used to flood the dry dock are connected to reach rods controlled by hand wheels at the top of the wing walls; the hand cranks control the movement of the side blocks.

PHOTOS: Michael Falco

Dry Docking

The deck of the dry dock

Counter-clockwise from right: The deck of the dry dock with bearers, bilge blocks, and wing wall; the wing wall with chains that connect to blocks; keel and bilge blocks; and a bilge block.

PHOTOS: Michael Falco

floating palaces. They were deteriorating below the waterline, and had to be repaired or they would be lost. His scheme to get at the parts of the vessels that were underwater was to erect pillars in the trench, lay heavy crosswise beams on them, and then open up the area from the lake to fill it with water. After they towed it in, workers could pump out the trench, rest the ship on the beams, and work on the hull. After they finished the repairs, they could let water in again, re-float the ship, and move it back down the trench into the lake.

In 1496 in Portsmouth, England, the nascent British Navy built the first enclosed dock from which water could be drained. In 1669 the French built *Vieille-Forme*, the first masonry dry dock set into the shore. An enclosed basin, it was fitted with watertight entrance gates that permitted the water to be pumped from the area. Charles II, sometimes called the Father of the Royal Navy, quickly followed in France's footsteps and built England's first stone dry dock at the Portsmouth Naval Shipyard in 1700.

The process of dry docking a ship speeded up at the turn of the nineteenth century, after the invention of the steam engine to power dry dock pumps. In 1801 British engineer Sir Samuel Bentham added another improvement; he designed and built the first caisson for the Royal Navy's graving dock. A caisson is a wooden box that serves as a gate between the sea and the interior basin of a graving dock. As the process begins, workers move the caisson away from the entrance. When the caisson has been removed, they shift the ship into the flooded basin. They then position the empty caisson at the entrance to the dock and fill it with water so that it sinks into slots built into the side of the dock and make a watertight seal. Then they pump out the basin of the dock dry.

Some graving docks are equipped with sliding side blocks, but in most, workers set all of the blocks to their final heights before the vessel comes into the graving dock. When it is ready to come out of the dock after repairs are complete, workers flood the basin through valves. When the water pressure on both sides is equal, they pump the caisson out and float it out of the way so that they can shift the ship out of the dock.

The floating dry dock is an outgrowth of the caisson concept. It is a "box" with two sides, called "wing walls." Built like a pontoon, it can be filled and emptied in order to raise and lower it. The two side wing walls provide buoyancy and stability to the box. Hand wheels connect to reach rods that open and close flood gates below the waterline to fill and empty, thus raising, or lowering, the whole box.

The dockmaster, who directs the dry docking, consults the docking plan specified by the marine architect who designed the ship. In the absence of a docking plan, he takes measurements from inside the ship's hull and references photographs and other drawings to develop one. Caddell's dockmaster keeps the hull measurements of each ship the yard services in a handwritten ledger. Each time a ship returns to the yard, he consults the ledger to build "side," also called "bilge" or "pull" blocks, to hold it up around its hull once the dock is emptied of water. He builds a cradle for the ship.

The essentials of the docking plan are the LOA, or the length overall of the vessel; the beam, or breadth of the vessel; the drafts, forward and aft, that indicate what portion of the boat is below waterline; the distance from the after-end of the vessel to the first side block and first keel block; the height and configuration of the side and keel blocks; and the bilge block spacing.

Before a vessel with a shaped hull comes into a floating dry dock, the dockmaster sets the keel blocks, which support most of the weight. He also builds the side blocks to stabilize the vessel and keep it in an upright position. He monitors the lowering of the dry dock by watching its gauge boards, also called "fingerboards," measuring devices at each end of both wing walls with draft marks to indicate the depth of the water over the keel blocks. If, for example, the draft of the vessel is seventeen feet, and the dockmaster needs one foot of clearance over the keel blocks, he submerges the dry dock to eighteen feet above the keel. Then he slowly pumps it out, and it rises. When it meets the keel blocks, it lifts the hull out of the water.

Not all vessels have shaped hulls; some have flat-bottomed hulls. Before a vessel with a flat or unshaped hull comes into a floating dry dock, the dockmaster sets the keel and side blocks according to the dead rise, or the difference between the height of the keel and the height of the bilge of the vessel.

The maximum hauling capacity of Caddell's dry docks is four to six thousand tons. When dry docking such a huge, heavy vessel, the dockmaster knows it is not stable on the keel blocks alone, although they take most of its weight. After he makes sure it is resting its keel from bow to stern, he directs workers to begin moving in the side blocks. He controls their movement with a series of pulleys and chains connected to the hand cranks at the top of the wing walls. As workers pull the chains, the blocks slide into position along the steel tracks, or "bearers," that are athwart the ship on the deck of the box. Then the dockmaster pumps out the dry dock until the vessel is completely out of the water.

Caddell's has one of the last wood dry docks in the world, dry dock #1, but wood dry docks are rapidly disappearing from the waterfront because they require constant maintenance. Dry docks made of wood cannot fully sink without some stone ballast, in addition to water, in the box. After many years, as the wood becomes waterlogged, they do, however, sink without ballast. Modern dry docks do not require permanent, fixed ballast because they are made of steel, which is heavier than wood, and sinks readily.

Although the main purpose of dry docking

is to make repairs to the parts of a ship that are normally underwater, repairs at the shipyard run a wide gamut. Hulls may need to be repaired, cleaned, and painted. Repairs to machinery that is below the waterline, such as a vessel's propulsion system, are common. Propellers, shafts, bearings, and rudders have to be "changed out," and modern systems, like outdrives that require specialized repair, have to be addressed. While the underwater parts of the ship are being worked on, Caddell's often addresses "overboard" repairs, or those that can be made while the ship is not on dry dock. They overhaul parts of a ship's interior, including its electrical, plumbing, and piping systems. The yard also does cabinetry, joinery, insulation,

1. Not submerged, the dry dock is set to receive a vessel with its keel and bilge blocks built. The flood gates have been opened, and it will gradually sink as the box and wing walls fill with water.

2. The dry dock is submerged, and the vessel has been shifted into it. The dockmaster has closed the flood gates, and the ship has been maneuvered over the keel blocks.

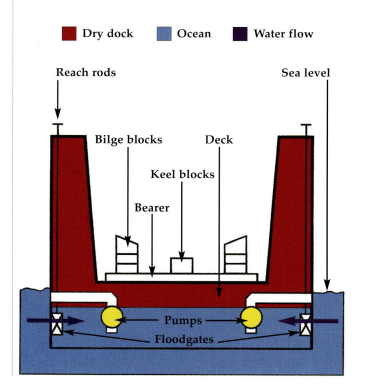

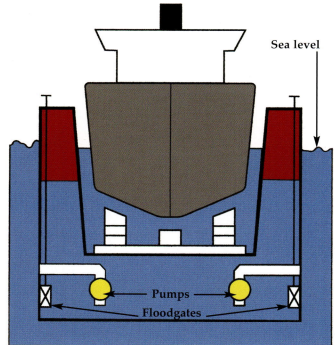

and steel work, and repairs and replaces fender systems while the ship is on dry dock as well as, when practical, after it is off dock.

After the shipyard crew completes the underwater repairs, they lower the dry dock back into the water, a process called "undocking." The dockmaster opens the flood gates and allows the dry dock to flood and re-submerge. When the vessel is afloat, he closes the flood gates. The yard tug pulls the ship out. The dockmaster starts the pumps and raises the dry dock back out of the water.

3. As the dry dock is slowly pumped out, the vessel slowly lands on the blocks.

4. The dry dock has been pumped out, and the vessel is out of the water resting on the keel and bilge blocks.

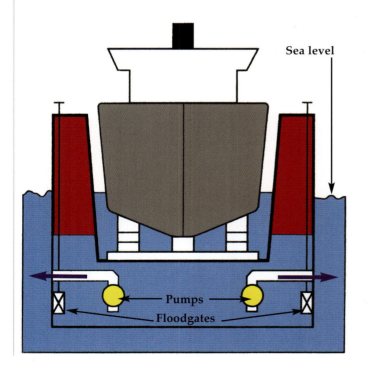

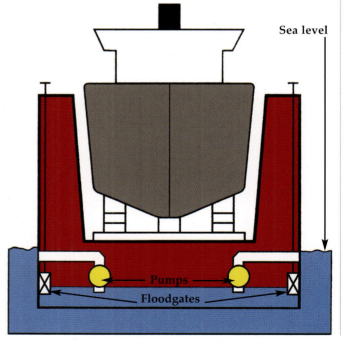

Portrait of a Dry Dock

Previous page: Dry docking the tugboat *Barbara E. Bouchard*; hauling out is nearly complete, and the vessel is about to clear the deck of the dry dock.

Right: The over 70 year-old yard storeroom and pier in Caddell's main yard. Claude Forbes managed the storeroom for over 40 years.

Portrait of a Dry Dock

In the fall of 2003, the Noble Maritime Collection, a maritime museum and study center located on the grounds of the famous old mariners' home, Sailors' Snug Harbor, commissioned photographer Michael Falco to document the hauling out of a ship at Caddell Dry Dock and Repair Company for the museum's upcoming exhibition *Caddell Dry Dock: 100 Years Harborside*. After clearing the way with John B. Caddell II and Steve Kalil, Falco spent three weeks at the yard and documented the hauling out of a tugboat, its repair, and its undocking. The yard is active around the clock, and Falco knew he would have to spend a great deal of time there, at night as well as during the day, and he did. As the men at the shipyard gradually warmed up to him, he pulled off layer after layer of their world, revealing the life of the ship below the waterline, and the relationships and dynamics of the yard crew.

Heating the tug's propeller with a kerosene heating torch.

Portrait of a Dry Dock
by Michael Falco

I had never been in a shipyard. I'd looked at Caddell's from a distance with photographer lust—I think every photographer feels the same way—and always wanted to get inside. When Erin Urban asked me to photograph it for an exhibition at the Noble museum, I was very excited. We went to Caddell's, met Steve Kalil, and coordinated things around the dry docking of the *Barbara E. Bouchard*.

I showed up at about seven in the morning on the day the tugboat was due. Groups of men were milling around, getting ready to start. A few were working on the dry dock; the rest were waiting to begin work. From that point on, it was a complete education for me.

I was awed by the size of the dry dock, which is actually a very simple, age-old mechanism that can work under harsh conditions. It's pulleys and blocks, and using water to its advantage. I was also struck by how everything they do at the shipyard is custom. There are no set formulas—every dry docking is unique—and dangerous—and done by "feel." The keel blocks are set, but the actual dry dock is underwater, and they can't see it when the boat comes in.

As I sat with Steve on the apron of dry dock #7, men on top of the wing walls kept the tug correctly positioned over the keel blocks while the yard tug *LW Caddell* towed the *Bouchard* into the submerged dock. The worker in my photo who sits watching the operation *(page 73)*, sits there every day as ships of one size and shape or another get hauled out, and even as a seasoned dock worker, he's glued to the action. Each time it's an event.

I tried to imagine the weight it was lifting as the dry dock came up very slowly out of the water. The side blocks were not set yet, and the tug had to rest on the keel blocks. The ship was huge—those "cute little tugs" are powerful machines, with massive engines—and when one comes up out of the water, the shipyard crew has to get it just right. And they get it just right by feel. One false step and the ship could topple over on to its side and destroy the dry dock as it goes down.

After that first morning Steve made sure I was wearing boots and a hard hat, but otherwise gave me free range of the yard. It's a dangerous environment, but he knows what it takes to get a good photograph.

It took three or four visits before things got comfortable. The men were slow to warm up to me. I was in their world, and it's not like a corporate environment, where there are rules. The dry dock is a private space, off the street, and behind fences. It's kind of like going to a different country with its own customs and rules. An outsider coming in stands out, and it took some time before I gained the trust of the yard workers. Some, of course, are characters—*hey, take my picture*—and others are all business—*don't point that camera at me*. The yard language is a ubiquitous dockside vernacular—twelve curse words, and everything can be determined by shifting those twelve words around. Columbians, South Asians, Africans, Chinese—they're tough-looking hombres, especially in grimy coveralls. Underneath, they're all sweethearts.

I went with my heart in my hand, observing, not taking a lot of pictures at first, getting them more comfortable with my being there, forgetting I'm there. You have to be there for awhile before you can step back and get a little bird's eye view that's true, and not stilted. Three or four visits, and some joking around—*hey, take a picture of the guy next to me*—and they became friendlier. I realized Cliff Fah Sang was most experienced and began to direct my questions to him. He understood what I was doing—a document—left me alone, and did not alter what the crew was doing to accommodate me. Gradually, as the men saw that I would hang around to catch a certain shot, they began to take me more seriously, and to direct me to certain events in the sequence of repair that was unfolding. As they realized I was interested, they let me know what they were going to do.

I was watching a kind of show—one that's careful and methodical. It's almost like playing with toys, but the toys are gigantic. Because so much is custom, it demands total attention and constant tweaking, using your eye to make miniscule adjustments. The *Bouchard* was getting, among other things, two reconditioned propellers. To install one, they had to heat it with a huge kerosene torch to expand it. When it was installed, it contracted around the tail shaft as it cooled, providing an ultra-tight fit.

When I met John Caddell I met another tough cookie, a man who never lets down his guard. His game face is all seriousness. He knew Erin and I were working on something together, so he gave me a little leeway. After I made him drag out the scaffolding for the big group portrait he wanted, and asked him to delay his trip to Florida so that he could be in it, and he saw me insisting on certain things, saw that I was doing it right, he too let me in. My goal is trust— untethered access—and to get that blessing from John Caddell made me feel honored.

It presented a challenge as well. He stuck his neck out for me—as did Steve and the men who let me into their world. You come with your hat in your hand. Their trust made me push myself, stay longer—*wait—they might move that*—I wanted to get each shot right. Let's face it, they're it. In New York Harbor, the Caddell guys are the cream of the crop. Who else is there? Who else can do what they do?

After measuring the bore of the propeller hub, the machinist notes its dimensions.

The *Barbara E. Bouchard* awaits repairs pierside.

Portrait of a Dry Dock

Above: The yard tug the *LW Caddell* is shifting the 1,000 ton, 6,000 horsepower tugboat *Barbara E. Bouchard* from Pier 2, where she was awaiting repairs, into dry dock #7.

Right: The tugboat has been shifted into the submerged dry dock.

Portrait of a Dry Dock

Dockmaster Domenico Spezzacatena, *left,* is in charge of dry docking, or hauling out, the vessel. Before a ship arrives, he consults its blocking plan and builds the keel blocks according to the specifications of the plan. Then he floods the dry dock so that the ship can pass into it. After the vessel is over the box, he pumps it out and slowly raises the ship on its keel. The most critical time in the dry docking operation comes when raising the dry dock is almost complete, and its deck is breaking the surface of the water.

Above: Hauling out is almost complete. The vessel is about to clear the surface of the water.

Right: The dry docking is almost complete; the vessel has been balanced on its keel.

Portrait of a Dry Dock

Workers have removed the port and starboard propellers and are setting up to remove the tail shaft.

Portrait of a Dry Dock

The *Barbara E. Bouchard* is in dry dock; the side blocks are in place as workers construct scaffolding around her hull.

Portrait of a Dry Dock

Caddell Dry Dock: 100 Years Harborside

Left: Machinist Nicola Spagnoletti

Above and right: Workers in dry dock #7 getting off and on the tug.

Portrait of a Dry Dock

Caddell Dry Dock: 100 Years Harborside

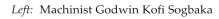

Left: Machinist Godwin Kofi Sogbaka

Above: Machinists rig the shaft out of the vessel.

Facing page: Machinists use a 150-ton jack to push the new stern bearing into the stern tube.

Portrait of a Dry Dock

Caddell Dry Dock: 100 Years Harborside

Portrait of a Dry Dock

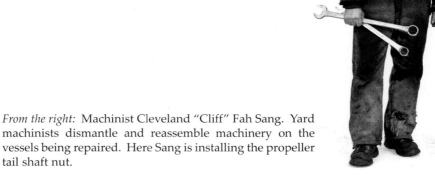

From the right: Machinist Cleveland "Cliff" Fah Sang. Yard machinists dismantle and reassemble machinery on the vessels being repaired. Here Sang is installing the propeller tail shaft nut.

Caddell Dry Dock: 100 Years Harborside

Left: Nicola DeVincenzo, machinist

Right: The new propeller is rigged, and the machinists prepare to transfer it by crane to the vessel.

Portrait of a Dry Dock

Left: The shaft is in place, the new propeller is rigged, and the machinists prepare to install it.

Top right: A machinist is cleaning the bore of the propeller.

Bottom right: Fah Sang inspects the reconditioned propeller.

Left: Ironworkers Adolfo and Raul Arellano have a variety of tasks in the shipyard. On the *Barbara E. Bouchard*, they removed and replaced the steel shelves that hold the bow fenders in place.

Above and right: They are in the process of fabricating new shelves for the tug's fenders.

Portrait of a Dry Dock

Caddell Dry Dock: 100 Years Harborside

Left: A welder is cutting off the old starboard bow fender shelves and brackets.

Above: Looking from the deck of the *Bouchard* in dry dock #7 towards dry dock #3, where the tug *Mister T* is being repaired. Behind the tug are the pier and the main offices.

Right: Welders are installing new fender brackets.

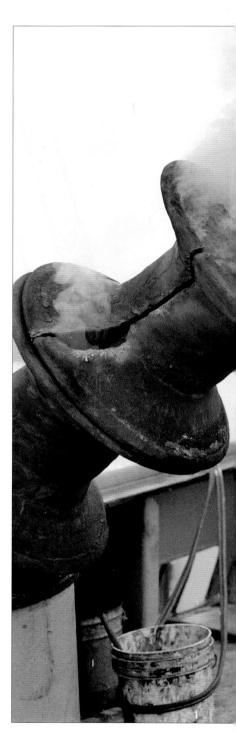

Top left: Born in 1934, Alfonso Rueda, one of the yard's carpenters, worked at Caddell's for twenty years. The yard carpenter works on vessels and on dry docks. He removed the paneling from inside the *Bouchard's* galley in preparation for welding and other hot work on the vessel's hull. He also built the staging that functions as a platform around a ship undergoing repair. After the ironworkers removed the old fenders and repaired the hull, the carpenter refitted the rubber fenders that cushion the tug when it is alongside a pier or another vessel. Rueda also routinely repaired leaks and damage to Caddell's wooden dry docks.

Bottom left: A worker is cleaning the forepeak ballast tank of the *Bouchard*.

Right: Most oceangoing tugs have towing machines which release the cable they use for towing; the *Barbara E. Bouchard* carries 2,200 feet of 2¼ inch cable. The Texas bar and Texas bar roller at top of the photograph are used as guides to keep the cable from damaging the stern of the tug.

Caddell Dry Dock: 100 Years Harborside

Portrait of a Dry Dock

Electrician Ricardo Hoffman replaces a light on a mast. On the *Barbara E. Bouchard* the electricians re-wired the navigation lights, which display the tow of the vessel, and repaired the capstan, a mechanized device used to handle lines.

Caddell Dry Dock: 100 Years Harborside

Left: Sandblasting the hull of the tug prior to painting it.

Above: The vessel has been painted; the new fenders are in place; the scaffolding is down, and workers are clearing the dry dock of sand blast grit before undocking.

Right: At pierside, a painter is putting final touches on the tugboat.

Caddell Dry Dock: 100 Years Harborside

Portrait of a Dry Dock

Preceding page: Morning at the shipyard, a view of dry dock #7 with the *Bouchard* tug, and to its right, workers on a spudded barge moored next to the Clyde crane barge.

Above: The tug is tied up to the pier to finish repairs like painting that can be done "overboard," or not on dry dock.

Right: The underwater portion of the work on the *Barbara E. Bouchard* is complete. The dry dock has been flooded, and the vessel is being taken off the dry dock, a process called "undocking."

Portrait of a Dry Dock

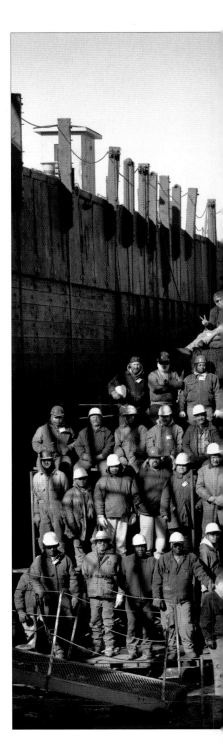

The shipyard workers aboard the Buchanan Marine LP tug *Buchanan 10*, February, 2004

Top level: Denys Springer, Raul Arellano, Michael Patrick, Andy Ammon, James Farrel, Isaac Rampersad, Cleveland Fah Sang, Angel DeLeon, Renato Romero, Gustavo Johnson, Dalton Milligen, Peter Bernard, Evangelista Contreras, Alfonso Rueda, Steve Blaize, Abraham Nieves, Baudilio Santiago, Daniel Gerhardt, Ramon Sanchez, Vinod Hiralal, Bryan DeFreitas, Dhaleep Singh, John Nichas, Aldwyn Walcott, Ephrain Small, Jailall Sanasie, Deodat Persaud, Nicola Spagnoletti, Rolondo Lodge, Luis Cepeda, Joseph Lazaro, Geronimo Toro, Pertab Singh, Jose Pereira, Carlos Salas

Lower left: Vincent O'Neill, Luis Inga, Orin Jonas, Pablo Burgos, Miguel Agosto, McDonald King, Celestino Varela, Bienvenido Nunez, Latchman Hiralall, Armando Garcia, Enrique Sosa, Ramon Rivera, Juan Urioso, Antonio Mendoza, Eric Ferrier, Antonio Mezzina, Clement Lall, Dogan Sahin, Luis Penafiel, Diego Castillo, Guy Smith, Yvon Auguste, James Barry, Damien Sundarsingh, William Rennie, Asen Georgieff, John Bereznak, Jackie Donovan, Paul Zbikowski, Mehmet Vataksi, Cynthia Pattelli, Ricardo Ramos, Latif Duraku, John B. Caddell, James Mullusky, Jennie DelPin, Kelvin Stokes, Kevin Trey, Domenico Spezzacatena, Arne Suppe, Richard Laverie, Wilson Guzman

Lower right: Steve Kalil, Gary Trivelli, Darlington Canmu, Nicola DeVincenzo, Parmanand Dhautal, Victor Castellon, Thomas Donato, William Doran, Robert Utize, Higgins Flanders, Vincent Gadaleta, Ricardo Hoffman, Fred Jasinski, Fitzroy Job, Carlos Jorge, Mostafa Hassan, Antonio Lemos, Bogdan Lipinski, Craig Litrell, Mario Markiewicz, Neville Marsh, Fitzroy Meade, Eddy Mondoza, Julien Meridin, Giuseppe Minutillo, Rafael Nunez, Richard Pawelkiewicz, Roque Pena, Andrew Peschier, Jose Rodriquez, Elliot Pressley, Eric Rampersad, Emil Rodriguez, George Roussis, Hamdi Salem, Edward Seecharan, Anthony Selman, Godwin Kofi Sogbaka, Hector Sosa, Peter Soverall, Ioan Sterp, Faustino Tejada, Luc Vaval, Hardyal William

Portrait of a Dry Dock

Bibliography and List of Sources

Looking up from the deck of dry dock #7 to the top of the wing wall. PHOTO: Michael Falco

Published works

Althenaeus of Naucratis (Yonge, C.D., Editor), *The Deipnosophists, or Banquet of the learned of Althenaeus*, Volume 1; London: Henry G. Bohn

Author unknown, "1936—Larsen Shipyard Sold," *The Staten Island Advance*, undated, c. 1937

Foley, Tom, *United States Gypsum, A Company History 1902-1994*; Chicago: USG Corporation, 1995

Hepburn, Richard D., P.E., *History of American Naval Dry Docks, A Key Ingredient to Maritime Power*, Arlington; Virginia: Noesis, Inc., 2003

Merlis, Brian and Rosenzweig, Lee A., *Brooklyn's Bay Ridge and Fort Hamilton, A Photographic Journey, 1870-1970*, Brooklyn, New York: Israelowitz Publishing, 2000

Needham, Joseph, *Science and Civilization in China*, Volume 4; Taipei: Caves Books, Ltd.

Paulsen, Ken, "North Shore was a haven for the rich," *The Staten Island Advance*, County Legacy, June 19, 1989

Ward, Nathan, "The Fire Last Time, When terrorists first struck New York's financial district," *Library Journal,* November/December, 2001, Volume 52, Number 8

Unpublished works

All quotations from John B. Caddell II and Steve Kalil are taken from taped interviews with the author in January, 1999, and in subsequent conversations that took place from October 2003 through January 2004, and from January through June, 2008. All quotations from Claude Forbes are taken from a taped interview with the author on January 28, 1999.

Steve Kalil, "New York Harbor Union Shipyards, 1961-2001," unpublished chart, undated

Ibid., "Dry Dock Operations Schematic," July, 2001

Martin Sr., Captain and Mrs. Jacob, Letter to John Bartlett Caddell II, October 19, 1963

Potts, Eva Mae, "The Old Hearthstone," Letter to John B. Caddell, May 10, 1949

xi	"…over the past half-century, over 30 working shipyards in the harbor…" Steve Kalil, "New York Harbor Union Shipyards, 1961-2001," unpublished chart, undated
12	…and Leroy remembered his "going to the shipyard and home by bicycle." John B. Caddell II, interview with the author
12	"I have just received a bill…" John B. Caddell, letter to Leroy Caddell, undated
28	"The Old Hearthstone" Eva Mae Potts, letter to John B. Caddell, May 10, 1949
30	Claude "…was one of the brightest guys I ever met…" John B. Caddell, II, interview with the author
32	"Mrs. Martin and I wish to thank you…" Captain Jacob Martin, letter to John Bartlett Caddell II, October 19, 1968
34	"Somebody is going to realize that moving things by water…" Steve Kalil, interview with the author, September, 2003
46	"Over-regulation is a real negative…" John B. Caddell II, interview with the author

Acknowledgements

Rarely do I visit the shipyard without a feeling of happiness and anticipation, even though I'm not, as John Caddell would say "sea friendly," and don't spend much time aboard ships. But the huge but hidden world behind the wall and fences, inside Caddell's, brings out my childlike wonder.

I'm sure I would never have ventured, much less been welcomed, into that world were it not for Steve Kalil. Patient and painstaking, he taught me about the shipyard and dry docking.

Behind him was John B. Caddell II, "the last man standing in the Harbor," as Peter Stanford called him when he persuaded him to do the book. He may have been reluctant at first, but he saw that there is truth in what Peter wrote. Caddell's is a preeminent firm in New York Harbor, exemplary in its work, its treatment of staff and customers, and its leadership of the maritime industry in this new century. I thank Mr. Caddell for allowing this book to go forward and nurturing it along the way. He has a long, precise, and illuminating memory. He financed this production, and will donate the proceeds to the Noble Maritime Collection.

Michael Falco puts his viewer into his photographs; you see the scene through his eyes, and you can feel it, and almost breathe it. He is exacting about every shot he takes, and each one stands the way he took it.

Dealing with these perfectionists, and me too, was a joy to Ciro Galeno, Jr., who has always been more than delighted to make this book better, through rewriting, through the discovery of new Falco photographs that could not be ignored, through the proofreading, correcting, and meticulous printing. His perfectionism is evident in the clarity and execution of the design.

I would like to thank Jill Cutler and Kris Fresonke for donating their talents to edit and clarify the document, and Coral Swofford for her careful proofreading.

Martha Keucher and Lois Duffy read and reread, corrected, and helped in invisible ways. I am honored that they donate their time and intellect to the museum.

Erin Urban
Snug Harbor, 2008

Index

A yard worker ascends the stairway in dry dock #1.
PHOTO: Michael Falco

Page numbers for illustrated entries appear in bold face type.

A

Admiral Dewey	xiv, 7, **8**, 29
Agosto, Miguel	102
allision	42
Althenaeus of Naucratis	52
Ambrose	34
American Shipyards	33
Ammon, Andy	102
Andrew J. Barberi	**3**, 42
Anne Moran	**26**
Anarchist Society	11
apron	15, 65
Arellano, Adolfo	88
Arellano, Raul	**88**, 102
Arethusa	37
Aron Foundation	37
Atlantic Salt Company	5
Auguste, Yvon	102
Austen class ferries	43

B

Barbara E. Bouchard	iv, **xvii**, **61**, 62, 65-66, **68-83**, **86-101**
Barry, Frank	22
Barry, James	102
Barwick, Kent	xiii
Baylies Shipyard	13
Bay of Fundy	**4**
Bay Ridge, Brooklyn	7, 12
beam	57
bearers	55, 57, **58**
Bentham, Sir Samuel	56
Bereznak, John	102
Bernard, Peter	102
Berwind White Coal Company	xiv, 7-9, 15, 18
Bethlehem Key Highway Shipyard	32
Bethlehem Steel Shipbuilding Division	5
Big Betty	**44**
bilge blocks	**53**, **55**, 57, **58-59**
Blairstown	xv
Blaize, Steve	102
Blue Room	13, 27
Borst, Joseph	**35**
Bouchard B. No. 242	**41**
Bouchard Transportation Company	3, 32
box	45, 57
breaming	51
Breezy Point Ferry	**22**
Brewer Dry Dock Company	31
Brighton Marine Shipyard	xv, 31
British Navy	56
Buchanan Marine	32
Buchanan 10	**102-103**
Burgos, Pablo	**102**
Burlee Shipyard	xiv, 5, 12

C

Caddell, Annie Forbes	4, **5**, 7, 12, **20**
Caddell, Archibald	9
Caddell, Beatrice	**5**, 7, 12
Caddell, John Bartlett (JB)	
Early years	xiii, 3-4, 52
Erie Basin years	xiv, **5**-7
Staten Island years	7-9
Late years	**10**, 11-12, 15, **20**, **28**, 47
Caddell II, John Bartlett (JBC)	
Early years	xv, **28**, 30
Education	30
Company president	xv, **30**, 31-32

Index

Chairman and CEO 32, **33**, 34, 46-47, 66, **102**
Caddell, Laura 5, 7, 12
Caddell, Leroy
   Early years 5, 7, **12**
   Education 12-13
   Naval career **12**, 13
   Chairman and CEO 11, 13-15, 20, 23, **27-28**, 30, **31**
Caddell, Lillian 5, 7, 12
Caddell, Marjean 7, 12
Caddell, Raymond 9
Caddell, Ruth Nordenholt 27
Caddell, William 4
caisson 56-57
Canmu, Darlington 102
careening 51
Carrol Towing Company tug 16
Castellon, Victor 102
Castillo, Diego 102
Cepeda, Luis 102
Charles II 56
Chin-ming Lake 53
Circle Line 22
Clair, Frank 22
Claude Forbes viii
Clements, Betty (Caddell) 44
Clyde crane barge **98-99**, 100
Contreras, Evangelista 102
Craig Reinauer viii

D

DeFreitas, Bryan 102
Delaware and Lackawana Railroad 31
DeLeon, Angel 102
DelPin, Jennie 102
DeVincenzo, Nicola **84**, **102**
Dhautal, Parmanand 102
docking plan 56
dockmaster 56-59
Donato, Thomas 102
Donjon Marine 32
Donovan, Jackie 102
Doran, William 102
Driscoll, Jerry 22
dry dock #1 viii, 7, **21**, 31, **45**, **51**, 109

dry dock #2 7, 15, 16, 31, 33
dry dock #3 iv, **xvii**, **17**, **18**, 31, 33
dry dock #4 **23**, 31, 33
dry dock #5 31
dry dock #6 32, **37**, **40**, **41**, 44
dry dock #7 **ii**, iv, **xvii**, 33, **49**, 50, **70-80**, **83**, **86**, **88-89**, **91**, **96-101**
dry dock #8 viii, 33, **47**
Dunlap, Charles E. xiv
Duraku, Latif 102

E

Eagle (USCG Eagle) 38
East Yard **3**, 31
Eastport of New York 6
Edward J. Berwind xiv, **15**
Elams, Artie 34
Elizabeth Moran 35
Erie Lackawana Railroad 45
Erie Basin xiv, 5, **6**, 7, **52**
Esso (Standard Oil of New Jersey) 9
Esso #7 xv
Esso #8 xv
Esso motor tanker 29
Esso Tug No. 11 **24-25**
Eureka 18
Evening Star viii
Export of New York 6
Exxon 9

F

Fah Sang, Cleveland 66, **82-83**, **85**, **86**, 87
Falco, Michael xvi, 63
Farrel, James 102
fenders, bow iv, **88-91**
Ferrier, Eric 102
fingerboard **54**, 57
Flanders, Higgins 102
floating dry dock 57
flood gates 56, **58-59**
Flying P Line 37
Forbes, Annie 4, **5**, 7, 12, **20**
Forbes, Claude 8, **30**, 62
Forbes, Wentworth 5, 8, 31
Frederick Lundy 22
French, Captain William xiv

G

Gadaleta, Vincent 102
Garcia, Armando 102
gauge board **54**, 57
Gazela of Philadelphia **34**, **36**
Gazela Primeiro (Gazela of Philadelphia) 36
General Contracting Company 29
Georgieff, Asen 102
Gerhardt, Daniel 102
Glory **29**, 32
Governor's Island ferry 22
graving 52
graving dock **52**, 56
Gulf of Maine xiii
Guy V. Molinari 43
Guzman, Wilson 102
Gypsum Queen 5

H

H & R Dry Dock Company xiii
Half Moon 34
Hassan, Mostafa 102
Heaney, Jim 27
Hightstown xv
Hildebrant Dry Dock Company 7
Hiralal, Vinod 102
Hiralall, Latchman 102
HMS Rose (see *Rose, HMS*)
Hodgdon Yachts, Inc. 32
Hoffman, Ricardo **94-95**, **102**
Horst Wessel 38
Hudson River Line 29
Hughes Brothers 33

I

Inga, Luis 102

J

Jasinski, Fred 102
Jay Bee 29
Jay Bee II 29
JB V viii, 37
Job, Fitzroy 102
John A. Noble ferry 43
John B. Caddell **20-21**

Index

John B. Caddell Dry Dock
    Company   7
Johnson, Gustavo   102
Jonas, Orin   102
Jorge, Carlos   102

K
K-Sea Transportation   32
Kalil, Steve   ix, xvi, 32, **34**,
     46, 63, 65-66, **102**
keel   58
keel blocks   52, **53**, **55**, 57, **58-59**
Kennedy Class ferries   43
Kill van Kull   xiv, 7
King, McDonald   102

L
Lake Elsinore   6
Lall, Clement   102
Larsen Shipyard   xv, 15
Lane, Bill   27
Lawrence Shipyard   4
Laverie, Richard   102
laying a ship aground   51-52
Lazaro, Joseph   102
Lemos, Antonio   102
Lipinski, Bogdan   102
Litrell, Craig   102
Lodge, Rolondo   102
LW Caddell   **viii, 47, 70**

M
M. & J. Tracy   26
Maitland, Nova Scotia   4
Maple Grove, Nova Scotia
     3, 4, 12, 28
Marshall McCoy   14
Marine Power and Light
     Boat Yard   **xiii, 3**
Maritime Museum of San Diego
     39
Markham Homes   29
Markiewicz, Mario   102
Marsh, Neville   102
Martin, Captain Jacob   29, 32
Master and Commander:
     The Far Side of the World   39

May Ship Repair Contracting
     Corporation   47
McAllister Towing and
     Transportation Company, Inc.
     26, 32
Meade, Fitzroy   102
Mendoza, Antonio   102
Meridin, Julien   102
Merrill, Ralph   30-32
Meurot Club, St. George,
     Staten Island   13, **27**
Mezzina, Antonio   102
Milligen, Dalton   102
Minutillo, Giuseppe   102
Miss New Jersey   51
Mister T   iv, **xvii**, 91
Molinari Class ferries   43
Mondoza, Eddy   102
Moran Towing & Transportation
     Company   32
Morton S. Bouchard   viii
Mullusky, James   102
Municipal Art Society   xiii

N
New York & Cuba Mail
     Steamship Company   6
New York Waterways ferries   22
Nichas, John   102
Nieves, Abraham   102
Noble, John A.   xi
Noble Maritime Collection
     xi, 63, 65
Nordenholt, Ruth   27
Nova Scotia   3-5, 28
Nunez, Bienvenido   102
Nunez, Rafael   102
NYC Dept. of Environmental
     Protection Sewage Treatment
     Plant   3

O
"Old Hearthstone, The"   28
O'Neill, Vincent   102
Op Sail 2000   36
overboard repairs   58, 100

P
Patrice McAllister   26
Patrick, Michael   102
Pattelli, Cynthia   102
Pawelkiewicz, Richard   102
Payne, John   5
Peking   34, **37**
Pena, Roque   102
Penafiel, Luis   102
Penn Maritime Transportation
     Company   xiii, 32
Pereira, Jose   102
Persaud, Deodat   102
Perth Amboy Dry Dock   27
Peschier, Andrew   102
Philadelphia Maritime Museum
     36
Poling & Cutler Marine
     Transportation   20
Poling, Mrs. Carol   **20**
Poling, Chester A.   17, 20
Poling, Robert   20
Poling Transportation Company
     20, **29**, 33
Port Jefferson ferries   22
Portsmouth Naval Shipyard   56
Potts, Eva Mae   28
Pressley, Elliot   102

Q
Quinlan Oil   29

R
Ramos, Ricardo   102
Rampersad, Eric   102
Rampersad, Isaac   102
reach rods   54, **58**
Red Hook   5
Reinauer Transportation   32
Reliable Fuel Company tanker   **17**
Rennie, William   102
Rhea L. Bouchard   viii
Rivera, Ramon   102
Rodriguez, Emil   102
Rodriquez, Jose   102
Romero, Renato   102
Rose, HMS   39
Roussis, George   102

Rueda, Alfonso **92, 102**

S
Sahin, Dogan 102
Salas, Carlos 102
Salem, Hamdi 102
Saluda 6
Sanasie, Jailall 102
Sanchez, Ramon 102
Sang, Cleveland Fah 102
Santiago, Baudilio 102
Schuyler, Eugene 5, 7
Schuyler and Caddell 5, 7
Schuyler, Payne & Caddell
 5, 6, 12
Seecharan, Edward 102
Selman, Anthony 102
Sen. John J. Marchi 43
Shen Kuo 53
side blocks 54, 56, **76-77**
Singh, Dhaleep 102
Singh, Pertab 102
Small, Ephrain 102
Smith, Guy 102
Smith, William Wikoff 36
Socony (Standard Oil of
 New York) 9
Sogbaka, Godwin Kofi 80, **102**
Sosa, Enrique 102
Sosa, Hector 102
South Street Seaport Museum
 34, 37, 40
Soverall, Peter 102
Spagnoletti, Nicola **78, 102**
Spezzacatena, Domenico 72, **102**
Spirit of America 43
Springer, Denys 102
spur shores 52
Stacey 8
Standard Boat 33
Standard Oil Company 9, 29, 33
Stanford, Peter ix
Starin, John 7, 9
Starin Shipyard 7, **9**
Staten Island Advance 15
Staten Island Ferry 22, 30, **42-43**
Staten Island Shipbuilding 5
Statue of Liberty Line 22, 51

Sterp, Ioan 102
Stokes, Kelvin 102
Sundarsingh, Damien 102
Suppe, Arne 102
Surprise 39

T
Tabeling, Harold 17
Tarantula 12, **13**
Tejada, Faustino 102
Texas bar 92, **93**
Texas bar roller 92, **93**
Tiejan & Lang Shipyard 5
Todd Shipyard 5, **52**
Toro, Geronimo 102
Tracy Towing Company
 9, 26, 27
Trey, Kevin 102
Trivelli, Gary 102

U
undocking 59, **100-101**
Urban, Erin ix, xvi, 65, 107, 113
Urioso, Juan 102
U.S. Coast Guard 9, 14, 33, 38
US Gypsum 5
Utize, Robert 102

V
Vanbro Sand & Gravel Company
 29
Vanderbilt, Commodore
 Cornelius 13
Vanderbilt, William K. 12, 13
Van Wee, John xiv
Varela, Celestino 102
Vataksi, Mehmet 102
Vaval, Luc 102
Vieille-Forme 56
Villa Restaurant, Stapleton,
 Staten Island 13, 27

W
Walcott, Aldwyn 102
Wall Street bombing 11
Ward Line 6
Washington Coyler 22
Wavertree xvi, 34, **40**

Weeks Marine 32
William, Hardyal 102
Windsor Plaster Mill 5
wing walls **54-55**, 57

XYZ
Yorel 32
Zbikowski, Paul 102

About the Author

Erin Urban is the founding executive director of the Noble Maritime Collection. With the help of an amazing corps of volunteers, the Noble Crew, she organized the restoration of a former mariners' dormitory at the famous old retirement home for mariners, Staten Island's Sailors' Snug Harbor. Volunteers transformed a derelict building into a spacious 28,500 square foot maritime museum and study center, the Noble Maritime Collection, named in honor of John A. Noble (1913-1983), the American painter and printmaker.

A graduate of Lake Forest College, Urban wrote and designed two books about Noble, *John A. Noble: The Rowboat Drawings*, 1988, a selection of *plein air* drawings; and *Hulls and Hulks in the Tide of Time: The Life and Work of John A. Noble*, the definitive biography and *catalogue raisonné*. She also wrote and designed *Bon à tirer: The Prints of Herman Zaage*, and helped produce the museum's book of museum manners for children, *The Terrible Captain Jack Visits the Museum or A Guide to Museum Manners for Incorrigible Pirates and the Like*, by Diane Matyas. Urban has put together several museum publications including *The Fight for Sailors' Snug Harbor*, 1995, a collection of Noble's essays and letters about the preservation of the Snug Harbor site, and *The Sailors' Snug Harbor Coloring Book*. She also wrote the script for the video documentary *Hulls and Hulks in the Tide of Time: A Portrait of John A. Noble*.

Since 1984, Urban has served as curator for exhibitions at the museum, including the restoration of Noble's houseboat studio and the installation of the permanent exhibition of his lithographs aboard the Staten Island ferry *John A. Noble*. The *Noble* is the only ferryboat in the country used for regular commuter commerce with a permanent art installation.

Urban is the proud mother of two sons, Damon and Samuel, and has lived on Staten Island for 30 years.